STEAL THE STREET

Working and Writing for Change
Series Editors: Steve Parks and Jessica Pauszek

The Working and Writing for Change series began during the 100th anniversary celebrations of NCTE. It was designed to recognize the collective work of teachers of English, Writing, Composition, and Rhetoric to work within and across diverse identities to ensure the field recognize and respect language, educational, political, and social rights of all students, teachers, and community members. While initially solely focused on the work of NCTE/CCCC Special Interest Groups and Caucuses, the series now includes texts written by individuals in partnership with other communities struggling for social recognition and justice.

Books in the Series

CCCC/NCTE Caucuses

Viva Nuestro Caucus: Rewriting the Forgotten Pages of Our Caucus ed. by Romeo García, Iris D. Ruiz, Anita Hernández & María Paz Carvajal Regidor

History of the Black Caucus National Council Teachers of English by Marianna White Davis

Listening to Our Elders: Working and Writing for Social Change by Samantha Blackmon, Cristina Kirklighter, & Steve Parks

Building a Community, Having a Home: A History of the Conference on College Composition and Communication ed. by Jennifer Sano-Franchini, Terese Guinsatao Monberg, & K. Hyoejin Yoon

Community Publications

Literacy and Pedagogy in an Age of Misinformation and Disinformation ed. by Tara Lockhart, Brenda Glascott, Chris Warnick, Juli Parrish, & Justin Lewis

Faces of Courage: Ten Years of Building Sanctuary by Harvey Finkle

Equality and Justice: An Engaged Generation, a Troubled World by Michael Chehade, Alex Granner, Ahmed Abdelhakim Hachelaf, Madhu Napa, Samantha Owens, & Steve Parks

Other People's English: Code-Meshing, Code-Switching, and African American Literacy by Vershawn Ashanti Young, Rusty Barrett, Y'Shanda Young-Rivera, & Kim Brian Lovejoy

Becoming International: Musings on Studying Abroad in America, ed.by Sadie Shorr-Parks

Dreams and Nightmares: I Fled Alone to the United States When I Was Fourteen by Liliana Velásquez. edited and translated by Mark Lyon

The Weight of My Armor: Creative Nonfiction and Poetry by the Syracuse Veterans' Writing Group, ed. by Ivy Kleinbart, Peter McShane, & Eileen Schell

PHD to PhD: How Education Saved My Life by Elaine Richardson

STEAL THE STREET
THE INTERSECTION OF HOMELESSNESS AND GENTRIFICATION

Mark Mussman

Parlor Press
Anderson, South Carolina
www.parlorpress.com

Parlor Press LLC, Anderson, South Carolina, USA
Copyright © 2022 by New City Community Press

No part of this book may be reproduced or transmitted in any form, by any means electronic or mechanical, including photocopying and recording, or by any information storage or retrieval system, without written permission from the publisher.

Printed in the United States of America on acid-free paper.

Library of Congress Cataloging-in-Publication Data on File

2 3 4 5

978-1-64317-327-6 (paperback)
978-1-64317-328-3 (PDF)

Working and Writing for Change
An Imprint Series of Parlor Press
Series Editors: Steve Parks and Jessica Pauszek

All photographs by Mark Mussman
Interior design by Justin Lewis, justalewis1@gmail.com

Parlor Press, LLC is an independent publisher of scholarly and trade titles in print and multimedia formats. This book is available in paper and eBook formats from Parlor Press on the World Wide Web at www.parlorpress.com or through online and brick-and-mortar bookstores. For submission information or to find out about Parlor Press publications, write to Parlor Press, 3015 Brackenberry Drive, Anderson, South Carolina, 29621, or email editor@parlorpress.com.

Dedication

I would like to dedicate this book first to my family and friends who have supported me throughout the years, including Key Beck, my partner, who has challenged my thinking and writing every step of the way. I would also like to dedicate this work to everyone at the Greater Cincinnati Homeless Coalition, including the Speakers, Melissa Mosby, Deonna Flowers, Willa Jones, Samuel Jackson, Lauren Lovett, Lee McCoy, and Cleo Wombles. My time spent with each of the Speakers has given me a deeper understanding of the urgency of solving our housing crisis, as well as a stronger understanding of the experience of homelessness. To all of the Staff, Volunteers, Board, and Supporters of the Homeless Coalition, this is also dedicated to you. Thank you for your support.

My family has been my most constant supporter in my life, and I would like to dedicate this to Aunt Lynn, you mean more to me than life itself. Thank you for giving me a shot in this world and never judging me or tearing me down. Your memory lives in all of us.

Finally, I would like to also dedicate this book to the many people who have come into and out of my life during the period when this was written: Catherine Comello Stehlin, Tom Dutton, Jawari Porter, Larry Files, and all of the residents who have been displaced from their homes in the name of progress. You are not forgotten.

CONTENTS

XI   FORWARD

XV   INTRODUCTION

1   Chapter 1: Background on Cincinnati History
            Cincinnati History Through the Great Depression
            Cincinnati and Urban Renewal
            Cincinnati Today

13   Chapter 2: Displacement in a Changing Neighborhood
            On Notice: Loss in OTR (5/6/2016)
            Acting and Action: To See or Not to See (6/3/2016)
            Side-Stepping Responsibility: Lessons from the Street (8/26/2016)
            Have We Confused Progress with Status Quo? (2/24/2017)
            No Country For All (5/5/2017)
            Hostile Design (5/19/2017)
            What's in a Name? (6/2/2017)
            Of Course It's Nice (6/30/2017)
            Donation Stations' Solution Conflation (8/11/2017)
            Double Trouble: Double Standards (9/22/2017)
            Institutional Racism Still Lives (10/6/2017)
            Out of Sight, Out of Mind? (10/20/2017)
            The Allure of Gentrification (2/9/2018)
            My Picket Line (2/23/2018)
            FC Cincinnati: Paternalism, Greed, and Racism, Oh my! (3/9/2018)
            Eyes On The City (3/23/2018)
            Do You Speak Like a Gentrifier? (4/20/2018)
            Read the Writing on the Wall (7/13/2018)

62   Chapter 3: Power Factors in the Community
The System is Broke (11/26/2018)
Push Back or Get Pushed Out (12/06/2018)
Keep an Eye On... (1/7/2019)
Wholly Unrecognizable (2/1/2019)
Segregation Now (2/14/2019)
Disappearing Communities (3/27/2019)
How to Bury a Story (4/11/2019)
Affordable For What? (5/13/2019)
Participatory Budget (6/20/2019)
Battle for Imagination Alley (07/05/2019)
The Big Squeeze (7/23/2019)
Barriers and Belonging (9/1/2019)
A Microcosm of Hypocrisy (11/20/2019)
It's a Wrap (11/11/2019)

120   Chapter 4: Systematic Loss of Community Cohesion
Politics of Protest (7/15/2016)
Singularity (7/29/2016)
Being Brave in Freedom Land (9/2/2016)
The Worst Is Yet To Come (4/14/2017)
Is a Picture Worth a Thousand Homes (7/7/2017)
Cincinnati's Crisis Mode (9/8/2017)
Police State Terror (5/4/2018)

138   Chapter 5: Homelessness and Gentrification
Counting On Us... (1/15/2016)
Sorry Not Today (4/11/2018)
Number 1 or Number 2 (5/18/2018)
Faking It (6/1/2018)
What City Hall Got Wrong (7/22/2018)
Cruel and Unusual Punishment (8/24/2018)
Know Your Rights! (10/5/2018)
It Couldn't Happen to Me (10/11/2018)
Underreported: Out of the Shadows (11/7/2018)
Boarded Up (3/7/2019)
Under the Law (5/2/2019)
Double Standards (8/8/2019)
Criminalization of Existence (9/16/2019)
I Didn't Even Know (9/30/2019)
An Altered State of Homelessness (10/25/2019)

180	Activity: Tactics of Gentrification: Photographic Neighborhood Assessment
183	Glossary
191	Study Questions
195	Acknowledgments
197	About the Author

Forward

Like many cities with urban, aging neighborhoods in the United States struggling with current iterations of economic development, discrimination, and gentrification, Cincinnati is no exception. Documentation of these struggles is found in several sources including the work of the Greater Cincinnati Homeless Coalition especially in publication of the street newspaper *Streetvibes*. The collection of articles written by Mark Mussman, the Coalition's Director of Education that follow here are drawn from *Streetvibes* - so named as it is published by the Coalition to be distributed on the street sold person-to-person by community individuals, not retail vendors nor coin boxes. During periods of deep socio-economic divisions, removal of affordable housing *and* neighborhood-friendly businesses are facilitated by privatization of City governance through economic and community development, and obdurate racial and economic discrimination. These accounts are uniquely positioned to reflect how such struggles evolve on the street, in the neighborhoods, in the lives of those who are economically poor, whose voices are rarely heard, whose daily realities are often unseen. While there is an abundance of available information about urban Cincinnati both written and oral found in newspapers, media reports, academic studies, economic and political research, education and arts institutional reports, even fiction and lawsuits, *Streetvibes* is unique.

Several historic eventualities need be cited here to fully understand the nuances of "Steal the Street" published in *Streetvibes*.

- The locus and focus of much of the conflict and discrimination found herein historically originates in the neighborhood known by the epithet "Over-the-Rhine." The iconic name derives from German immigrants to Cincinnati in the 1840's settling in the Ohio River basin just north of the Miami-Erie Canal (now a major east-west street Central Parkway) north of the Ohio River and Central Business District but below the hillsides to the north. Soon to be a densely populated German-speaking community accommodating residences, businesses, substantial housing, and many breweries, what might have been named "Germantown" or

"The Brewery District" in other locations, the ethnic slur Over-the-Rhine was a convenient moniker.

- As there were many, many breweries and saloons in Over-the-Rhine that became of significant interest in the era of Prohibition when, as the legend goes, Carrie Nation and her axe-yielding crusaders on a mission to smash the windows of saloons gave up in frustration in Over-the-Rhine - "I would have dropped from exhaustion before I got to 12th Street...but two blocks north of the 'Rhine'."

- Over-the-Rhine's solidly built, multifamily buildings (known more recently as the largest collection of Italianate architecture in the US) were densely packed in five Census Tracts housing a population of 15,025 in the 1970 Census, soon to become home to thousands of single adults released from state hospitals up and down Interstate I-75 with the "deinstitutionalization" triggered by the *Community Mental Health Centers Act of 1963*. 88-164. These new neighbors had lived in state hospitals for years, some decades and were thrown into Over-the-Rhine, many living in spaces that were known in the 'hood as SRO's- single room occupancy. These newly arrived residents were soon reviled, many became "homeless," later among the first to be removed from Over-the-Rhine (Skirtz, 2012). By 2010 the population was 7,422 after the removal of several "undesirable" populations and most of the affordable housing in the name of economic development.

Fast forwarding to 2001 in previews of coming community strife, discrimination, and neighborhood violence, the Cincinnati Police Department shot and killed teenager Timothy Thomas as he fled on foot jumping over a backyard fence in Over-the-Rhine. Community furor was instant outrage and civil disturbance. Many refer to this episode as the "Riots of 2001," Mark uses terminology of "the Rebellion." It is important to note that just days before this police shooting, a law suit was filed against the City of Cincinnati and the Fraternal Order of Police for the killing of *fifteen* men – Timothy Thomas was the sixteenth. This was nearly 15 years before Black Lives Matter organizing and advocacy evolved throughout the country.

    The collection of columns that follow here are a compendium of interpretation and reflection on matters affecting the community drawn in ways never accessible to the majority press, scholars, and others who have no contact with those who are poor, experience homelessness, nor are targets of discrimination by race, gender, or economic means. In short, they enable all to access the realities of several often-unseen communities – those who are victims of discrimination, homelessness, and exclusion.

A note about the author, Mark Mussman, Ph.D. known in several neighborhoods with affection and respect as "Dr. Mark" – a title by which both his academic credential (PhD) and his presence in and service to the community are recognized. His work with the Homeless Coalition enables many community folks to participate in a larger dialogue affirmed by his expertise and made honest by his presence with several communities – academic *and* on the street.

Alice Skirtz, PhD, LISW-S
Author, *Econocide: elimination of the urban poor* (2012)

WORKS CITED

Bronson, Peter. 2006. *Behind the lines: the untold stories of the Cincinnati riots.* Milford, OH: Chilidog Press.

Dabney, Wendell P. 1926. *Cincinnati's colored citizens: historical, sociological, and biographical.* Cincinnati, OH: The Dabney Publishing Company.

Bechtel, Judith A. and Robert M. Coughlin. 1991. *Building the beloved community: Maurice McCrackin's life for peace and civil rights.* Philadelphia, PA: Temple University Press.

Fairbanks, Robert B. 1988. *Making better citizens: housing reform and the community development strategy in Cincinnati, 1890-1960.* Urbana and Chicago, IL: University of Illinois Press.

Skirtz, Alice. 2012. *Econocide: elimination of the urban poor.* Washington, DC: National Association of Social Workers Press.

Suess, Jeff. 2015. *Lost Cincinnati.* Charleston, SC: The History Press.

Taylor, Henry Louis, Jr. 1993. *Race and the city: work, community, and protest in Cincinnati, 1820-1970.* Urbana, IL: University of Illinois Press.

Tolzmann, Don Heinrich. 2011. *Over-the-Rhine tour guide: Cincinnati's historic German district, Over-the-Rhine, and environs.* Milford, OH: Little Miami Pub. Co.

Introduction

The need for the compilation of these articles is clear as Over-the-Rhine is constantly being studied by scholars, students, think-tanks, and the community at large. Over-the-Rhine is a neighborhood immediately adjacent to the Downtown Business District in Cincinnati. Many American cities are facing rapid displacement of Black residents by white suburban wealth. Over-the-Rhine, and its surrounding neighborhoods of the West End, Mt. Auburn, CUF, Pendleton, and Walnut Hills, are no different than the neighborhoods across the country that are seeing rapid demographic changes.

In Over-the-Rhine, most of the Black residents have been removed in the past 15 years. Much of the removal has been directly related to the decisions of the local and state governments, who are clamoring for the development of previously neglected areas. Often the view of progress neglects the history of the area, and more egregiously, the residents. Property values are more important to the City than low-income residents who do not boost the City's income tax revenues.

In order to expedite the wholesale removal of Black residents from Over-the-Rhine, the City has offered no-strings-attached funding and tax benefits to developers, such as Tax Abatement, worth millions of dollars. Cincinnati has the distinction of being one of the most economically divergent cities, and the split between Black and white income and wealth is so vast that often the City is seen as having two distinct parts: one white and one Black.

However, it's the clash of cultures that enables Black residents to be devalued. Gentrification should always be understood as having an anti-Black bias, and should never be seen as a value-neutral endeavor. Economics include race. History includes race. And we cannot separate race from gentrification, just as we are seeing the impact of displacement almost exclusively within minority communities in America. In Cincinnati, however, the minority Black community makes up nearly half of the city's population, but is being removed from the City altogether.

Steal the Street is a collection of articles that were published in *Streetvibes*, a local street paper, published by the Greater Cincinnati Homeless Coalition. From 2015 through 2019, as the Director of Education, I produced over one hundred articles about various topics, including gentrification and displacement. Some of my articles and images are presented in the book in hopes that they will help to preserve the rich cultural heritage of Over-the-Rhine, as the residents face rapid displacement from the neighborhood. It is also a hope of mine that this will serve as a reference point for further research. As a resident of Over-the-Rhine, I was able to provide an insider's perspective on the gentrification of the neighborhood, but as the reader will find in the About the Author, my perspective is severely altered by my race and economic background.

In the first chapter, a summary of the people's history of Cincinnati is presented. This background provides the reader with a historical strand of injustice and exclusion that is uniquely Cincinnati. I have included links to additional publications in order to give the reader an opportunity to find additional voices on these topics. Following the history section, Chapter 2 largely focuses on big ideas to immerse the readers in the struggle of a neighborhood to retain its identity. Chapter 3 continues the focus on the struggle by looking more deeply into the power structure of the area. Chapter 4 looks at theoretical concepts that situate the neighborhood in a larger context, while Chapter 5 focuses on homelessness more directly; although the topic of homelessness and the loss of affordable housing are implicit throughout the book.

Finally, Chapter 6 briefly explicates tactics of gentrification that are used to displace residents and local businesses. In the end, it is the responsibility of those who have power, those who have gained generational wealth through homeownership, those who have benefited from the color of their skin, to stop and listen to residents, to lobby the City to fight for Black families, and to fully understand their power in white supremacist, capitalist, America. If we continue to purport solutions that don't provide housing, don't provide a path out of collective poverty, we will be at odds with our neighbors and ultimately, with justice.

CHAPTER 1: BACKGROUND ON CINCINNATI HISTORY

CINCINNATI HISTORY THROUGH THE GREAT DEPRESSION

It has been said that Cincinnati has always been a city of immigrants, but perhaps it should be rewritten as a city of homelessness. Going back nearly 40,000 years, people have always lived among these seven hills. The Hopewell, Shawnee, Adena, and Osage were just some of the people who lived here before the invasion.[1] There were major earthwork mounds and other features that were created over the span of tens of thousands of years. In a matter of a hundred years, we destroyed all the evidence in the downtown basin. The Cincinnati Tablet was found near the Shelterhouse's new location, on Mound Street, but all the other evidence has been removed.[2] Even Bald Knob, a sacred place, was removed for the infill of Union Terminal. To the south, the Cherokee and Chickasaw, among others, lived in the hills of Kentucky before they were removed. The French and Indian War ended in 1763, and the removal process started shortly after that. In 1788, Cincinnati was originally colonized as Losantiville, which combined several languages to mean "the city across from the Licking River." In 1819, "Cincinnati" officially became the city's name, named after a Roman general and farmer, and the society that bears its name.

For many years, Cincinnati was geographically smaller than downtown today. With Fort Washington near the location of the Taft Museum, all the area to the north was known as "Indian Territory" and was considered unsafe to travel, as Native Americans were being attacked, killed, and captured in order for the invaders to take the land which would eventually become Cincinnati. Our policies have always pushed people into homelessness. Less than a year after Ohio became a state in 1803, Ohio enacted the Black Codes, which required all Black people to register with the local magistrate, have two white people vouch

---

1 Charles Cist (1841). *1841 Census*. E. Morgan and Co. Power Press. Pages 25—27.

2 Cincinnati Museum Center: https://www.cincymuseum.org/2019/06/09/the-story-of-the-cincinnati-tablet/ Accessed 10/20/2020.

for them, and pay a hefty sum, just to live in Ohio.[3] Ohio used that money to build and create systems of oppression for Black people that continue to exacerbate homelessness. Ohio was literally built upon the backs of Black people as these laws were in effect until 1849, just one year after the mass migration out of Europe began.

By mid-century, Cincinnati was poised to grow into the first large inland metropolis in America.[4] In 1848 a social movement in Europe began. Seeking our First and Second Amendment rights, the "Forty Eighters" left Europe for North and South America, as well as Australia.[5] More than 30,000 Germans settled here in Over-the-Rhine (before it was called that), and built the buildings we still have today. Over-the-Rhine has the largest collection of German Italianate architecture anywhere in the world because the World Wars largely destroyed the buildings in Germany. The Germans came here, homeless, with little wealth, but many trade skills. Candle and rope making, beer and wine producing, masonry and woodworking, were some of the opportunities that the immigrants had. There was great conflict between the "Nativists" and immigrants. The white Nativists felt superior. Even though their idea of "native" had nothing to do with Native Americans, they acted as if they were more worthy of the land here. In addition, Black people, who were barred from owning land or even protection through the courts, also experienced institutional barriers. There was even an election day conflict that involved shooting a cannon over the canal. In contrast with Irish immigrants, the Germans more quickly became "white" and were able to fully participate and benefit from societal advantages.[6]

Up until World War I, schools, newspapers, books and other publications were in the German language. Many schools were bilingual, German and English. During the War, street names were changed (Bremen became Republic, Frankfort became Connecticut, Berlin became Woodrow, Hamburg became Stonewall, Hanover became Yukon, etc.), people were deported, and it is said that it became "illegal to speak German" in Cincinnati.[7] After the War, the US weathered the Great Depression, and Cincinnati's location along the river helped it stay afloat with cheap transportation. When it comes to housing, the Great Depression has shaped the United States more than almost anything else.

---

3 Black Past.org https://www.blackpast.org/african-american-history/1804-ohio-black-codes/ Accessed 10/20/2020.
4 Charles Cist (1851). *Cincinnati in 1851*. WM. H. Moore & Co. Page 34.
5 https://en.wikipedia.org/wiki/Forty-Eighters Accessed 10/20/2020.
6 Charles Rosebrough (2015). *Catholic-Protestant Relations in 19th Century Cincinnati*. https://www.exhibit.xavier.edu/cgi/viewcontent.cgi?article=1003&context=hab Accessed 10/20/20.
7 Ohio History Marker https://www.hmdb.org/m.asp?m=134945 Accessed 10/20/2020.

The Cincinnati that we know today was a result of Great Depression programs and post-war efforts. Even today, you can find WPA stamps on bridges, roads, playgrounds, schools, and other important developments. The Great Depression also set a minimum wage (except for tipped employees, incarcerated individuals, and people with developmental differences), which was supposed to be enough to buy a home, send your children to school, and put food on the table. If minimum wage kept up with inflation—the cost of living—the hourly rate would be over $22 today.[8] Contrasting that with the federal minimum wage of $7.25, which Kentucky follows, it's clear to see that the minimum wage needs to become a livable wage.

But there's one thing that came out of the Great Depression that's not so obvious, and that's the home ownership program that created the suburbs that we know today. Most housing in Cincinnati was built when housing discrimination (based upon race) was still very much legal and practiced widely. The federal home ownership program was notoriously racist, as Black people were described as if they were vermin requiring walls to keep out of white communities.[9] The resulting Redlining shaped our city and country. From 1934—1970, the federal government gave out $120 billion in low-interest, fixed-rate loans to build the suburbs. Over 98% of the loans went exclusively to white people to build generational wealth. Even though there was a generally level playing field after the Great Depression since very few had money, Black people were excluded from the home ownership program, denying them the opportunity to create generational wealth, or even housing stability. Today, we continue to feel the effects of this discriminatory practice as Black people are more likely to experience homelessness and have overall much less family wealth. Coupled with contemporary racism, Black people in Cincinnati face many barriers and obstacles.

---

8 Nick Wing (2013). *Elizabeth Warren: Minimum Wage Would Be $22 An Hour If It Had Kept Up With Productivity*. https://www.huffpost.com/entry/elizabeth-warren-minimum-wage_n_2900984 Accessed 10/20/2020.
9 George Lipsitz (1995). *The Possessive Investment in Whiteness: Racialized Social Democracy and the "White" Problem in American Studies*. The Johns Hopkins University Press. Pages 372-274.

CINCINNATI AND URBAN RENEWAL

The majority of housing in Cincinnati was built before 1970.[10] This means that while some housing has modern amenities, much of the housing was built before electricity, modern wiring, or even sewer systems (as in the case in Over-the-Rhine and the West End). The 1960's and 70's represented the tail end of the Great Migration of American Black families moving out of the South, and going as far north as possible. Unfortunately, once they arrived, they were still under the control of local jurisdictions who were not advocating for a free and equal society. The shadow of Jim Crow, the Black Codes, and segregation, were heavy in urban areas, like Cincinnati. Little had changed since the 1940's, when very few, if any, of the major corporations in Cincinnati had hired even a single Black person to work.[11] Another great migration was coming out of the Appalachian mountains, coal miners were being replaced by machinery, and they became unnecessary. On top of these two groups, both Black and white, there was another type of displacement that was occurring: Urban Renewal.

In Cincinnati, one of the greatest neighborhoods to be lost was Kenyon Barr, which is now the West End and Queensgate.[12] This neighborhood is to the west of downtown Cincinnati. The neighborhood was the epicenter of the Black community in Cincinnati. It was known as a "mixed income" neighborhood, with the bosses living on the same block as the workers. There was a long history of struggle and success, including Millionaire's Row (Dayton Street), and the more seedy places around the intersection of Kenyon and Barr Streets. Some of the first Black schools started here and later moved to Walnut Hills and other neighborhoods. When Kenyon Barr was razed for the West Side Highway, now I-75, it was just one of many Black neighborhoods that were destroyed, including Buck Town,[13] due to the lack of value Cincinnati whites place on the lives of Black residents. Over 25,000 Black people were forced out of Kenyon Barr, virtually overnight, because Cincinnati's white ruling class wanted the highway to come closer to the downtown, rather than stay on the Mill Creek.

By the mid 1960's, there were three groups of people (Great Migration, Appalachian, and Kenyon Barr residents) who were expelled from their homes and landed in Over-the-Rhine only to find the living conditions to be substandard, with many buildings containing many apartments without heating,

10 LISC (2020). *Housing Our Future: Strategies for Cincinnati and Hamilton County, May 2020.* Page 9.
11 Henry Louis Taylor (1993). *Race and the City: Work, Community, and Protest in Cincinnati, 1820-1970.* Pages 2-3.
12 HOME (2007). *Going Home: The Struggle for Fair Housing in Cincinnati 1900-2007.* Page 8.
13 Leonard Harding (1967). *The Cincinnati Riots of 1862.* The Cincinnati Historical Society. Page 238.

electricity, and even bathrooms. Some apartment buildings shared a single bathroom on the ground floor. The five story tenement buildings were already seeing degeneration and disinvestment, and the families who were displaced to Over-the-Rhine weren't in any economic position to obtain ownership of them. Several slumlords owned hundreds of properties each, including one immigrant from Lithuania who considered Black people "two legged horses" and disregarded the humanity of African Americans in Cincinnati. Slumlords let the buildings deteriorate while taking what money they could from the residents, often forcing residents to flee from one slumlord to another. Once again, the instability of housing was having a dire effect on the ability of Over-the-Rhine's 30,000 residents to gain a foothold for their children.

People in the neighborhood started to understand that ownership of the land was the only way that they could remain in the neighborhood to create stability for the next generations. They saw the need for social service organizations to help people who were being excluded from quality services, education, health care, housing, and shelter. Cincinnati, once known as the "City of Steeples," because of the many churches in the urban basin (which includes Over-the-Rhine and the West End), became a catalyst for community organizing. In the church basements, residents and clergy gathered to meet the economic and social crises head-on. Knowing that people needed to have better quality housing, they created ReStoc, which worked for decades to preserve old buildings for affordable housing. They created the Over-the-Rhine Housing Network, an organization to obtain and manage low-income and subsidized housing. They created the Shelterhouse because they recognized that Cincinnati needed a low-barrier shelter. They knew advocacy was important, so the Contact Center and the Homeless Coalition were created to push for systems change. In the ensuing years, other organizations were created like Peaslee Neighborhood Center, and religiously-influenced organizations like Tender Mercies, Power Inspires Progress (Venice on Vine), St. Francis Seraph's outreach programs, Mercy Housing, and the Mary Magdalen Shower House. The tireless efforts put into these life-giving organizations constitute what we now call the Over-the-Rhine People's Movement.

Each of these organizations has seen opposition from the City of Cincinnati and other fronts. For example, it is illegal to create a shelter in the city, so after buddy gray's apartment was too full for persons homeless, and the roof caved in at the Main Street building that was being used as a shelter, the city forcibly removed the shelter from the Teamster building at 12th and Elm. This happened several times before they were able to get the permit to keep the shelter there. The struggle to get Peaslee into the hands of the people was years long, and involved the untrained labor of mothers who didn't want to lose an important asset in their neighborhood. When Over-the-Rhine Housing Network and ReStoc knew that the Recovery Hotel was needed, the City denied the permit, yet the community came together and found a workaround, which enabled the Recovery Hotel to open.

Even as the population continued to decline into the 1990's, the People's Movement remained steadfast in their commitment to the quality of life issues of residents in Over-the-Rhine. But they were up against a federal designation: Historic Neighborhood. Residents had fought this designation because they knew this would result in less affordable housing and more displacement from the neighborhood, and they were absolutely correct. Developers had long fought the People's Movement, and the apparent leader, buddy gray, for entrée into the neighborhood. Developers and other business interests felt that the work of Urban Renewal was yet to be complete, so they set their sights on Over-the-Rhine, as it abuts the downtown business district. With the largest collection of 19th Century German Italianate architecture in the world, developers were eager to create a new neighborhood under the guise of "mixed income." They began with Main Street, which had been home to many people for decades. 80-year-old women were being taken out of their apartments, handcuffed, face-down, on stretchers, by the Sheriff, so that their apartments could be turned into condos for the wealthy, white, elite. The neighborhood was able to stem this tide, after many trips to City Hall demanding that these developers be held accountable for their apparent crimes against humanity. Unfortunately, accountability did not last.

CINCINNATI TODAY

People look back at Over-the-Rhine in the year 2000, and call it things like an economic wasteland, a drug infested slum, or the most dangerous neighborhood in the country.[14] It's clear that these comments come out of a certain group of people who wish to exert ownership, or who feel they weren't making money off of the approximately 8,000 residents. Many underground economies exist because of racist drug policies, or even racist permitting processes. Even though Over-the-Rhine was considered these negative things, there were many small mom-and-pop businesses, and even some larger, like Gold Star Chili, Kroger, Devaroes, yet most of the businesses catered to people who lived in Over-the-Rhine. Hair and nail salons, corner stores, hardware, art, post office, bars, clothing, and Findlay Market were places that residents found refuge in a world that was uncaring and difficult to them. Over-the-Rhine still had the Urban Appalachian Council[15] headquarters on Walnut Street, which was the first stop for many migrating families out of eastern Kentucky, West Virginia, and Tennessee. There were three elementary schools, a couple of private schools, and a public high school. The arts were thriving in the neighborhood, which seems to be a precursor for gentrification.

In April of 2001, there was a catalyzing event that brought the focus back onto Over-the-Rhine: the execution of Timothy Thomas by Cincinnati Police Officer Stephen Roach. The aftermath of this event led to a complete change in the way of life in Over-the-Rhine. After Stephen Roach killed 19 year-old Timothy Thomas, as Thomas fled down a dark alley in the middle of the night, Thomas' mother, and many other mothers and community leaders, went to City Hall to get answers about what happened. Thomas had been one, of more than a dozen, unarmed Black men killed by the Cincinnati Police in a few years. The mothers and grandmothers demanded to know why, and how they could protect their children. Unable to get a direct answer from the Police Chief, or any elected official, these concerned residents left City Hall, only to be greeted by riot police. This is what sparked the Rebellion in 2001, which is the largest city rebellion in recent American history.

After a chaotic few days, the Cincinnati Police decided to do a "slow-down" and abandoned the neighborhood. Some residents believe that this is

---

14 Colin Woodard (2016). *How Cincinnati Salvaged the Nation's Most Dangerous Neighborhood.* https://www.politico.com/magazine/story/2016/06/what-works-cincinnati-ohio-over-the-rhine-crime-neighborhood-turnaround-city-urban-revitalization-213969 Accessed 10/20/2020.
15 Phillip J. Obermiller and Steven R. Howe (2000). *Urban Appalachian and Appalachian Research in Greater Cincinnati: A Report.* https://uacvoice.org/docs/researcharchive/workingpapers/workingpaper16.pdf Accessed 10/20/2020.

when outside forces were able to take hold in the neighborhood, and this is why the neighborhood became known as the most dangerous neighborhood in the country. It is due to the complete economic breakdown that was occurring because of systemic racism and the oppression of low-income residents, coupled with an unjust legal system, and the lack of access to quality healthcare and education. Most crime that occurred was on paper—drug deals, etc., but there were strings of homicides, due to the fact that the police let it be known that they were not going to be patrolling or responding in Over-the-Rhine. People in the neighborhood were working together to create a stronger neighborhood, and for many, life continued as normal.

At the time, the Drop Inn Center (Shelterhouse) was still operating daily on 12th and Elm, providing meals for people, and shelter at night. Peaslee's Steel Drum Band was in full swing. Streetvibes was being published with the legendary Jimmy Heath at the helm. The Homeless Coalition was fighting against unjust panhandling laws and encampment sweeps. The Contact Center was registering people to vote and fighting against the Welfare to Work policies of the Clinton Administration. The Intercommunity Justice and Peace Center (at the time, the Interfaith Justice and Peace Center) was gearing up for a many-year fight against the illegal and unjust War on Terror. Mercy St. John was providing meals twice a day out of their sandwich windows. The Catholic Worker House was merging and providing a substance-free new beginning to men who needed short-term housing. And all the while, the Mary Magdalen House provided showers, clean clothing, and dignity to our neighbors from their storefront location on Main Street.

The operations of the Over-the-Rhine People's Movement could not be stopped because the need was so great. Nightly curfews over the city were applied only to Black and low-income residents, as parties and bar operations continued in Mt. Adams, Hyde Park, and other affluent neighborhoods. Mayor Charlie Luken told everyone to "go home and watch tv" and the nights became quiet around the edges of Over-the-Rhine. Before Officer Roach was acquitted of the misdemeanor charges brought upon him, the 2001 attacks took place on September 11th. This event changed the trajectory of the organizing in Cincinnati, as everyone was impacted by the event, no matter where you lived in the city. Once 9/11 happened, the passion around fighting for justice seemed to fizzle out, and people began to focus on systemic changes.

The federal Department of Justice (DOJ) came to Cincinnati and found that the Cincinnati police had been training their officers to use racial profiling as the base of their operations. Timothy Thomas had been pulled over many times for driving without a license, due to racial profiling. The DOJ required the Cincinnati Police to change policies,[16] which wasn't the first time the Cincinnati Police were required to change, as they were required to hire women and Black officers back in the 1980's due to the pervasive level of racism in the department.[17] After 2001, the police began to participate in Community Problem Oriented Policing (CPOP) only because members of the Black community fought to see systemic change. Due to the pressure from Black citizens and the Department of Justice, a Citizen's Complaint Authority (CCA) was created and police are to keep Contact Cards (information estimating the age, race, gender of everyone they come into contact with during their shift). The Fraternal Order of Police (FOP) has fought these changes many times, and often is out of compliance. The CCA keeps a record of police officers who are known to be racist, yet they have little power, due to the FOP.

Mayor John Cranley has said that the killing of Timothy Thomas, or as he inaccurately calls it the Race Riot of 2001, was the catalyst of the renaissance of Over-the-Rhine. But it's clear that the white ruling class had been conspiring to take control of the neighborhood since the 1980's, if not earlier. (Just a note: Race Riots have always been when white people destroy and kill people in Black neighborhoods. Calling the Rebellion in 2001 a "Race Riot" is entirely racist. Calling it a Civil Unrest is slightly better, but we know "Rebellion" is accurate because the DOJ showed unequivocally that the Cincinnati Police Department was operating unjustly, and rebellions are fights against injustice.) It was only after the Rebellion in 2001 that the Mayor at the time, Charlie Luken, and a Vice President of Procter and Gamble (P&G) colluded to create a extrajudicial organization that would have little to no governmental oversight: Cincinnati City Center Development Corporation, also known as 3CDC.

3CDC has become the largest purveyor of direct and indirect gentrification in Over-the-Rhine since it's entrance into the neighborhood around 2008. Before 2008, 3CDC briefly operated as the City's Planning Department due to funding cuts, used public funds to build the parking structure at the Banks for an entertainment district, and privatized Fountain Square in downtown Cincinnati. 3CDC paid as little as $1 for leases on city property, including Fountain Square, and later, Washington Park.

---

16 Alana Semuels (2015). *How to Fix a Broken Police Department*. The Atlantic. https://www.theatlantic.com/politics/archive/2015/05/cincinnati-police-reform/393797/ Accessed 10/20/2020.
17 Kevin Grasha and Sharon Coolidge (2018). *1980s court decisions at the center of racial divide lawsuit involving Cincinnati Police*. The Cincinnati Enquirer. https://www.cincinnati.com/story/news/crime/crime-and-courts/2018/06/14/suit-1980-s-court-decisions-caused-cincinnati-police-racial-divide/702594002/ Accessed 10/20/2020.

3CDC has directly removed low-income and Black residents from their homes, as well as small businesses. 3CDC has indirectly removed Black and low-income residents from the neighborhood entirely. We have seen a loss of more than half of the Black residents since 2001, and the trend continues today.[18] 3CDC's idea of affordable housing is not attainable to the residents, and only continues to further push residents from their homes. They operate as a quasi-governmental organization, with a backdoor to City Hall, where they are able to get millions in public funding that could be used to create and sustain affordable housing. 3CDC does not consider low-income people as their base because their board is hand-picked by the Mayor, and their membership is mostly Fortune 500 companies like Kroger, 5/3 Bank, P&G, and Macy's. They have no regard for low income families, unless they are asking the public for donations. As a private non-profit organization, they operate as a shadow government, which not only gets funds from all sorts of public sources but also directly from property taxes. In 2019 and 2020, they are working to expand their ability to receive property taxes directly,[19] as they have an insatiable thirst for power and control over the neighborhood.

Fortunately, the many founders of the Over-the-Rhine People's Movement had the foresight to own their property to create stability in the neighborhood. These organizations are continuously fighting back against the abuse of 3CDC, but because 3CDC has very little public oversight, it is a daunting task and struggle. Over-the-Rhine Community Council, a public neighborhood group, often votes against 3CDC proposals, but Cincinnati City Council overrides the community council wishes, or 3CDC just does what they want anyway. Until City Hall challenges, rather than protects, 3CDC, it will continue to be an uphill battle to fight for the rights of Black and low-income residents in Over-the-Rhine.

---

18 Katz, Black, and Noring (2019). *Cincinnati's Over-the-Rhine: A Private-Led Model For Revitalizing Urban Neighborhoods.* https://drexel.edu/~/media/Files/nowak-lab/NowakLab_3CDC_CityCase_web.ashx?la=en Accessed 10/20/2020.
19 OTR South Special Improvement District. https://www.otrsouthsid.com/ Accessed 12/27/2020.

WORKS CITED

Blackpast.org: (1804) *Ohio Black Codes.* https://www.blackpast.org/african-american-history/1804-ohio-black-codes/ Accessed 10/20/2020.

Cincinnati Museum Center: *The Story of the Cincinnati Tablet.* https://www.cincymuseum.org/2019/06/09/the-story-of-the-cincinnati-tablet/ Accessed 10/20/2020.

Cist, Charles (1841). *1841 Census.* E. Morgan and Co. Power Press. Pages 25-27.

Cist, Charles (1851). *Cincinnati in 1851.* WM. H. Moore & Co. Page 34.

German Forty-Eighters, Wikipedia entry, https://en.wikipedia.org/wiki/forty-Eighters Accessed 10/20/2020.

Grasha, Kevin and Coolidge, Sharon (2018). *1980s court decisions at the center of racial divide lawsuit involving Cincinnati Police.* The Cincinnati Enquirer. https://www.cincinnati.com/story/news/crime/crime-and-courts/2018/06/14/suit-1980-s-court-decisions-caused-cincinnati-police-racial-divide/702594002/ Accessed 10/20/2020.

Harding, Leonard (1967). *The Cincinnati Riots of 1862.* The Cincinnati Historical Society. Page 238.

HOME (2007). *Going Home: The Struggle for Fair Housing in Cincinnati 1900-2007.* Page 8.

Katz, Black, and Noring (2019). *Cincinnati's Over-the-Rhine: A Private-Led Model For Revitalizing Urban Neighborhoods.* https://drexel.edu/~/media/Files/nowak-lab/NowakLab_3CDC_CityCase_web.ashx?la=en Accessed 10/20/2020.

Lipsitz, George (1995). *The Possessive Investment in Whiteness: Racialized Social Democracy and the "White" Problem in American Studies.* The Johns Hopkins University Press. Pages 372-274.

LISC (2020). *Housing Our Future: Strategies for Cincinnati and Hamilton County,* May 2020. Page 9.

Obermiller, Phillip J. and Howe, Steven R. (2000). *Urban Appalachian and Appalachian Research in Greater Cincinnati: A Report.* https://uacvoice.org/docs/researcharchive/workingpapers/workingpaper16.pdf Accessed 10/20/2020.

Ohio History Marker https://www.hmdb.org/m.asp?m=134945 Accessed 10/20/2020.

OTR South Special Improvement District. https://www.otrsouthsid.com/ Accessed 12/27/2020.

Rosebrough, Charles (2015). *Catholic-Protestant Relations in 19th Century Cincin*

nati. https://www.exhibit.xavier.edu/cgi/viewcontent.
cgi?article=1003&context=hab Accessed 10/20/20.

Semuels, Alana (2015). *How to Fix a Broken Police Department.* The Atlantic. https://www.theatlantic.com/politics/archive/2015/05/cincinnati-police-reform/393797/ Accessed 10/20/2020.

Taylor, Henry Louis (1993). *Race and the City: Work, Community, and Protest in Cincinnati, 1820-1970.* Pages 2-3.

Wing, Nick (2013). *Elizabeth Warren: Minimum Wage Would Be $22 An Hour If It Had Kept Up With Productivity.* https://www.huffpost.com/entry/elizabeth-warren-minimum-wage_n_2900984 Accessed 10/20/2020.

Woodard, Colin (2016). *How Cincinnati Salvaged the Nation's Most Dangerous Neighborhood.* https://www.politico.com/magazine/story/2016/06/what-works-cincinnati-ohio-over-the-rhine-crime-neighborhood-turnaround-city-urban-revitalization-213969 Accessed 10/20/2020.

CHAPTER 2: DISPLACEMENT IN A CHANGING NEIGHBORHOOD

ON NOTICE: LOSS IN OTR
5/6/2016

Sometimes I feel like I'm punishing myself. Living, working, and focusing my life around Over-the-Rhine is a difficult and relentless existence. I am a very emotional person, guided by a sense of justice and beauty. What is balanced brings me joy, and right now, I feel no joy about Over-the-Rhine. My story is long and complicated, and for right now, doesn't feel wrapped up nice and tight. This is a meandering walk through my current struggle – the struggle for a peaceful existence.

In our neighborhood today, a young artist, a budding revolutionary, calls me to tell me that he is being evicted because his name wasn't on the lease. He and his roommates have less than 24 hours to vacate the premises. They have nowhere to go, thrust out of Over-the-Rhine, as there are no options here now. Peaslee has been working on showing just how many housing units we've lost in the past 15 years – a number that is staggering, yet still unclear. Affordable, or market, the number of housing units available has decreased significantly. Where is the renaissance for the artists?

Yesterday, as I walked past the basketball courts on 13th, the devastation has begun, and the construction workers got their parking lot. No more basketball court. A place where people played even in the cold winter, running laps around the lot, and occasionally picking up a game of 3 on 3 to stay warm. This spring saw a lot of friendly activity on the court. We have lost basketball courts to development. One simple question will answer why: Who uses basketball courts?

Last week, a fence was placed in front of Imagination Alley. Over 300 Over-the-Rhine residents, mostly children, spent a hot summer creating the mosaics that you see on the walls, ground, planters, and arch on Vine Street. This was a project that I participated in, and now 3CDC has it fenced off, leaving us wondering what will happen to the space in the near (or distant) future. Will we be able to access our community work?

In Washington Park last month, a huge tree fell on the dog park fence just feet from where Joann Burton was killed. Remnants of the tree still mark the fence posts. Just a month before that, another 100+ year-old tree was removed from the 13th street entrance to the park. Looking at the trunk, it seemed healthy. People fought to keep the trees in the park before, during, and after 3CDC's renovation. Why was it removed? Did they remove the wrong one?

Walking up Pleasant Street, on my way to Findlay Market, I noticed the "Field of Greens" park, which was used last summer by our kids, was also fenced off. Of course, we knew this was coming, as new condos will be built on the entire block, but it still doesn't lessen the impact when I see it. The center of the block will be a surface parking lot, with condos on the Race, 14th, and Pleasant sides of the block. It may be a small lot, but it was one where kids would play while listening to their own music, without having to follow the strict rules of Washington Park. Where can they listen to their own music now?

Hopefully, you have seen the push to Keep Our Courts, in the paper and even in video online. The #KeepOurCourts campaign started last year when developers were rewarded a preferred developer status for the block across Main Street from Rothenberg Elementary. The City, in all its infinite wisdom, wants to sell a city block for $1 to build $600,000 single family homes on it, in a neighborhood where the average income is just $12,000/year. This land was the first donated to create Cincinnati Public Schools. The development put on it will pay reduced taxes for up to 30 years, which means the schools will not receive full property taxes on the parcel. Why do we think it's a good practice to shortchange our children?

We resist privatization because it represents a loss of community wealth.

ACTING AND ACTION: TO SEE OR NOT TO SEE.
06/03/2016

I've been running the numbers on our education program and I'm impressed with the work that the Homeless Coalition does each year. We have had hundreds of engagements including speaking engagements, *Streetvibes* Shadow activities, training, social justice walking tours, Final Fridays at buddy's place, and other education events. Sometimes I feel that the purpose of the events are so simple: to humanize homelessness and show people how Affordable Housing has a positive impact on our community. But, in reality, due to extreme bias against people in poverty, people of color, and other marginalized groups, our education program is met with opposition in some of the least likely places.

I really enjoy working with people in our community. I feel empowered when I discuss difficult topics such as gentrification because when you break it down for people, it becomes something that is easily understood. I'll admit that it's taken me a long time to understand how the process of vilification of poverty and displacement are carried out on such a large scale. I have been experiencing it as a member of the community for years – I remember when I taught GED classes, I had a student who lived in the Pendleton neighborhood of Over-the-Rhine. I saw that the Model Group set its sights on creating "Broadway Square" by purchasing several buildings and I knew the student would be displaced. It doesn't matter if Model Group bought the building, or if 3CDC plans a takeover of a block, but it's the collective will of developers who decide to make changes in the neighborhood. When 3CDC moved north of Liberty last year, developers were scrambling to get on the gravy train and bought up all of the buildings. This same push happened in Pendleton a few years ago.

I asked the student if they had made plans for when they are kicked out, and the student responded that it would never happen because "my landlord owns the building, grew up in the building, and would never do that to us." Within a month, the student stopped showing up for class, so I called and called, and finally got in touch. "My landlord sold the building!" the student exclaimed. What it is like for a single mother to pick up everything and move in less than 30 days, I cannot imagine. What it meant from our side, was that the student (who was very close to passing the GED) missed too many classes to continue the term, and had to restart a month later – after finding a new place to live, in a new neighborhood. The landlord did care about the tenants and helped them pay for their rent for a couple months, but that is very rare.

This occurred a few years ago, but it is happening around us as we speak. When we look at the reimagined Ziegler Park, we can see that the housing surrounding the park will be bought up and transformed from affordable to market rate housing. The precedent was set with Washington Park, and now Ziegler, which was a heavily used park by people in the neighborhood, and will

Demolition of Ziegler Park, including pool, for privatization.

now be transformed into a privatized area, with 24/7 private security. Some people will say "it's safer now" after it is redone, but the question I ask is "safer for who?" Black and Brown bodies are constantly patrolled by police and private

Ziegler Park Pool is demolished by 3CDC without adequate community input.

security. We know the system has, and continues, to destroy their lives by criminalizing the same behaviors that white people get away with behind closed doors. In Over-the-Rhine, the sidewalks are our front lawns, the parks are our backyards, the alleys are our shortcuts, and when each of these spaces becomes privatized, on top of our housing becoming market rate, then we have no place here.

The legacy of racism lives on in Cincinnati. 75% of African-American kids live below the poverty line. Income inequality based upon race is so real that the median income for whites is more than twice of what it is for people of color. But even though we live in poverty it doesn't mean we have no value, no culture. Just because the people in Ziegler Park couldn't afford $8 craft beers doesn't mean they don't have a place in our community. This is a concept that developers and some educators don't understand. Whatever you do, don't sit back and say "that's someone else's job" or "it's not *that* bad!" One person displaced should be enough to get you to act.

SIDE-STEPPING RESPONSIBILITY: LESSONS FROM THE STREET
8/26/2016

When I walk around Over-the-Rhine it's clear that changes are happening rapidly. I heard that this year, something like 30 businesses have opened up in the neighborhood already, with many more just around the corner. I have been following some of the liquor license requests, and it seems that there will be a bar on every corner by this time next year. Over-the-Rhine will eventually become the French Quarter of Cincinnati once the permit to carry liquor on the streets is approved by the state. But when the bars close and the tourists go home, it's a different story. Melissa Mosby, one of our Speakers for Voices of Homelessness, talks about how people choose to ignore the suffering that occurs in the neighborhood. "When the bars close down and everyone leaves, they don't see the person trying to find a piece of pizza in the garbage can, or picking up a cigarette butt from the ground." Melissa spent many years living on Jackson street in Over-the-Rhine. Melissa has seen both sides of humanity – those who acknowledge the situation and those who ignore or exploit others.

When she tells her story of living in the doorway of the Know Theatre, I imagine that some people think she lived inside the building, but in reality she slept outside, using a little alcove for some shelter. Her feet lay on the sidewalk, exposed to the elements. People stepping over her legs on their way to work, ignoring the situation that she is in. Embarrassed, trying to not show signs of vulnerability, Melissa quickly packs up all her belongings into her backpack and hides her "bed" (cardboard and a mat made of Kroger bags) into the bushes beside the theater, and then acts like she is just sitting there, normally, like anyone else. Her ego struggles between being strong enough for anything that life throws at her, and understanding her limits.

If you are lucky enough to have heard Melissa tell her story, you may have heard her tell this heartbreaking story. One night, while college students and the bar crowd sauntered down Main Street (a street packed full of bars), Melissa saw a few college students standing around the Mary Magdalen Shower House. The Shower House is a special place in Cincinnati – a place where anyone can get a shower and a change of clothes. They also wash your clothes and you can get them when you come back for a shower in the next two weeks. Melissa's experience at the Shower House is one of gratitude and dignity, and she has a special place in her heart for the people who run it.

Melissa slowly approached the group standing by the Shower House and quickly noticed what was happening – one of her friends was sleeping in the doorway and "these kids were taking selfies, pretending to lay down next to my friend so I stopped them and asked them if they thought it was funny, 'Are you gonna post that on Instagram? Are you gonna Facebook that? He is a human being, that could be you.'" Melissa has confided in me that she could not bring herself to tell her sleeping friend what had transpired. "What good would it do, Dr. Mark?" She has helped me understand that when you live on the street your self-esteem is rock bottom, and even letting someone know about this might cause more pain in an already difficult situation.

On any Thursday, Friday, or Saturday night it's difficult to navigate the sidewalks without being stuck between groups of drunk people. I find it difficult to get through even when there is no one on the streets because of all the sidewalk seating the bars and restaurants are putting up. Just last week, another one popped up on Race Street at Zula. Navigating the sidewalks (which until very recently didn't have ramps on the corners, and some alleys still don't have ramps) in a wheelchair or another assistive device must be almost impossible. Near the Coalition the space between the bar's outdoor seating and the parking sign is so narrow that only one person can walk through at a time. The outcropping of Zula destroys any continuity of the sidewalk and creates a very narrow walkway. This makes carrying groceries difficult through here as well. But, when the goal is to create as many bars as possible (Over-the-Rhine split into two entertainment districts this year, so that is why we are getting twice as many liquor licenses) the everyday life is pushed to the side for the benefit of the bars.

Years ago, the talk in town was all about "Walkable Streets" and "Form-Based Code." Over-the-Rhine is walkable to an extent, but as social service agencies get moved to the fringe of the neighborhood it becomes more difficult for people to access services. Many organizations have moved to the West End or Queensgate, miles from here. In the near future, the Contact Center will be moving to Elm Street, from its long-term home on Vine Street, so that a business can move in. The AA/NA meeting space next to it at the Recovery Hotel will also be converted into a business. The Shower House is planning a move as well to a more accommodating building outside of the business district. Since so many other organizations have been removed from the neighborhood, only a few are left. One organization that is trying to keep services in the neighborhood is St. Francis Seraph, who is expanding their operations to include others who have been displaced like Haircuts from the Heart – and possibly the Shower House, but they can't absorb them all.

We are beyond the tipping point in Over-the-Rhine and it's going to take a lot of citizen input to ensure the neighborhood remains a community. If the current trend of displacement continues, this will be an exclusively rich, white neighborhood. For those coming in, parking at the 3CDC parking garages, bar hopping, and leaving, they may be happy for the removal. For those who do not believe that homelessness exists, for those who believe that every panhandler is lying about their need, for those who are willing to humiliate people who are struggling to live another day, they are complicit in the suffering that they are willing to ignore as they step over the feet of someone sleeping in a doorway.

SHAME IN THE CITY: HAVE WE CONFUSED PROGRESS WITH STATUS QUO?
2/24/2017

Between the years of 1934 and 1962, the United States federal government (FHA) issued more than 120 billion dollars in home ownership loans. These loans went to build the suburbs that we have today, and created much of the wealth that Americans enjoy today. If you grew up in a house, you most likely have these loans to thank for that. The loans enabled Americans to build wealth generationally and exponentially. People of color, regardless of economic status, were denied participation in the program through "redlining," which ultimately created a very uneven playing field.

In redlining, lines were drawn (on maps) around non-white communities and federal loans did not penetrate into those communities. Even as I write this, it seems like it was unintentional that people of color were left out of the loans, but redlining should be seen as completely intentional, because it was – less than 2% of the homeownership loans were given to people of color.

When we talk about concentrated poverty, we must also focus on concentrated wealth. The wealthy suburbs were created with restrictive covenants (forbidding the sale of property to non-whites), redlining, and de facto segregation. And none of this ended in the 1960's – it continues today with banks that participate in discriminatory and illegal activity. It also continues in other places like the courthouse, retail outlets, credit cards, mortgages, health care, student loans, environmental racism (DAPL). Today, our federal expenditures are more directed to supporting the housing secure, not the housing insecure.

When Cincinnati's West End (Kenyon-Barr) neighborhood was razed to the ground in the late 1950's, residents were told to leave their homes. Here was a whole neighborhood, sustained by African-Americans – many of them had bought themselves and their families out of slavery – full of life, wealth – a truly mixed-use and mixed-income neighborhood.

When Cincinnati decided that we wanted a way to get to the new shiny whites-only suburbs more quickly, we built a highway through the West End. Not the federal government, but us. We decided to tear down a whole neighborhood, almost exclusively African-American, without a real plan to deal with the displacement. Many were displaced to Avondale and other neighborhoods – most certainly to Over-the-Rhine.

Recently, I hear people arguing that the gentrification taking place in Over-the-Rhine right now is just "progress." It's clear to me that they are confusing "progress" with "status quo." Is it progress when powerful people throw people of color (and people in poverty) out into the street – or is this just the status quo? Is it progress when public goods (such as sidewalks, streets, parks, alleys, buildings, etc.) become privatized, or do we have enough of a grasp on neoliberalism to know that it is just the status quo of the late 20th Century? Is it progress when small businesses are closed and storefronts are left vacant for years? Or is this just another way that power shows itself?

As Over-the-Rhine shifts further into a bar and parking garage neighborhood, we must ask ourselves if the progress we are seeing is beneficial for our entire community, or is it just beneficial for someone else? As my neighbor put it yesterday – "Every time they build a parking lot, all it says is that we don't care about the quality of life, about the health, about the environment, in our community." She showed me how white flight hurts us all, and it seems to me that sprawl is probably the biggest cumulative environmental catastrophe of the 20th Century.

Since density is the future of city life, progress may be in the process of removing our grocery store from the neighborhood. This is where I get my cereal, milk, bread, produce, and snacks. This is where families in the neighborhood shop – mainly because the next closest grocery store is miles away.

The demographics in Over-the-Rhine are changing dramatically, with new housing coming in for wealthy residents coupled with the wide-scale loss of low-income housing. The new residents, with their cars and parking garages, jump on the highway, cross the river, and shop at the Newport Kroger. This isn't an option for many of us - nor should it be seen as a desirable one.

Across Vine Street from our grocery store, Kroger, is where Smitty's Men's Fashions was before the fire. Now, there are a few buildings vacant and a few lots empty. Currently, there's a fence around the sidewalk as another project gears up to fill the void with condos, shops, etc. Rumors started circulating late last year, after a Neighborhood Safety Meeting, where it is rumored to have been suggested by someone invested in the new development, that closing Kroger will deter undesirable street activity, such as drug dealing. To even suggest closing Kroger, our only grocery store, only to change what some people who don't live here (yet) will "see out of their windows" when they move in, is a sobering example of the gentrification of Over-the-Rhine. That this would be seen as a viable option for someone shows the disconnect between developers and community members.

Displacement doesn't require emotional labor. Displacement doesn't require solutions. Displacement doesn't require building bridges. Displacement *is* the status quo – it is not progress. So, before someone states that they are glad for the progress in Over-the-Rhine, remind them that progress is on the backs of more than 2300 low-income families who have been displaced out of the neighborhood in the last 15 years. This is on the backs of small business owners and non-profits that have been pushed out. This is at the expense of the schools who lose money on new development tax abatements. That it is with the loss of public spaces.

This progress may just be the powerful wringing what they can out of the powerless until they have had their fill. This is not progress in the true sense, but simply a continuance of the status quo – sustaining white supremacy.

[*Streetvibes* Editor's Note: On February 15, 2017, a member of the Kroger Media Relations/Corporate Communications Office confirmed that Kroger has no plans to close the store at this time. Over-the-Rhine Safety Sector meeting notes or minutes are not currently available.]

Rear view of incoming condos on Vine Street with Kroger grocery store in the background.

NO COUNTRY FOR ALL
05/05/2017

Yesterday, as I walked up Race Street, between 12th and 13th, I saw the most odd and disturbing thing. Generally, things are pretty peaceful there but there was a squirrel and a bird engaged in a violent fight. The bird swooped down from the treetop and swiped the side of the squirrel as it ran down the trunk. The squirrel was thrown off the tree and landed on the concrete. Brushing itself off, it head back up the tree as the bird violently swooped at it again. Why were these animals acting like this? I could only guess they were both vying for the same space.

It was clear that this was a turf battle to me, but I wasn't sure why, until I casually glanced over to Washington Park and saw another large, 100+ year-old, tree was cut into pieces on the ground. Either the squirrel or the bird was displaced from this tree, and it was causing chaos in the animal world. 3CDC, which has a lease on the park, has cut down several of the trees in Washington Park in the past year. They cite "disease" as the reason to cut them down, but I am seeing something more sinister with this last tree that was killed.

Underneath this now-gone tree, was a sanctuary of sorts for neighborhood residents and their friends to sit and enjoy the day. The benches under the tree have been removed (perhaps replaced soon?) but the effect of removing these benches was apparent to many. Were they asking the mostly Black bench-sitters to find a new place to gather – already regulated to the outside perimeter of the park? This is just one tree and several benches that were removed – think about the burden that housing displacement places on individuals, families, and communities.

Displacement might as well be our country's battle cry. Starting with the Native Americans, we have been displacing whole groups of people for generations – but this certainly does not make it right. Manifest Destiny is what it was called – white people who believed that they were given this land by their god (whether Christianity or Capitalism) which emboldened them to burn the forests and clear the land of people who lived here for at least 14,000 years. We had three major native-constructed earthen mounds here in downtown Cincinnati (including one on Fountain Square, now a privatized 3CDC space, not a public square) which were raised to remove the existence and record of the indigenous people. We white Americans saw no need to learn from, or even respect, the cultures of the Native Americans.

Fast forward ahead to the displacement of the people who lived in the Milner Hotel, the Dennison, the Metropole. Each of these SRO's (single room occupancies) provided low cost housing for many of downtown's service workers. Whether they clocked out as a janitor, a server, a bartender, or even as a white collar worker, there was a place for them to stay downtown. When the Metropole was closed by 3CDC to eventually create the 21C Museum and Hotel, residents were given very little time to vacate the premises. Once all of them were forcibly removed from the property, downtown lost its nationally recognized designation as a diverse community – resulting in a lawsuit which brought a small settlement, but the damage had already been done, residents were removed from their homes and their neighborhood.

Displacement is occurring at a rapid pace in Over-the-Rhine, fueled by the work of 3CDC, which is deemed the city's "preferred developer." When they entered the neighborhood about 10 years ago, they took over the entire block on Race, between 14th and 15th. They forcibly removed the residents and claimed that displacing them was the best solution to the substandard housing they were living in. No one from 3CDC asked the residents what they wanted repaired or updated in their homes. They just gave them the boot. As they did the corner stores and the other businesses that residents relied on for their livelihood. Whether it be the elementary school, the Laundromat, or the Drop Inn Center, 3CDC's reign of displacement is on a grand scale, and is hardly something that should be touted as a positive change in the neighborhood.

Today, we are seeing massive displacement in the northern part of Over-the-Rhine. The so-called Brewery District folks are explicitly using NEP to push families out of the neighborhood by making "anonymous" complaints about minor aesthetic issues to the city. Model Group has bought dozens of properties around Findlay Market and is using different tactics to push people out, including refusing to turn the heat on during the winter in one building and telling other buildings that they are at risk of being closed by the federal government. When 80+ year old women are being forced out of their homes so that developers can make money, it becomes everyone's issue. This is why we need everyone to join the Homeless Coalition as we assist residents who are at risk of losing their homes.

If you want to know why the homicide rate is so high right now in Cincinnati, (higher than that of Chicago even), perhaps you need to look no further than displacement. When people are displaced from their block, whether their housing or their outdoor marketplace, they are forced to enter into someone else's turf, and as direct competitors, they shoot it out. People are so callous in this community to cheer when someone dies of a drug overdose, or to point out a shooting victim's arrest record, but they are silent when it comes to understanding structural racism and the growing violence of displacement.

Just as the bird and the squirrel are fighting it out right now, we have lost our collective home in Over-the-Rhine. We cannot simply put the onus of ending the violence on those who are involved in the underground economy – we must dismantle the racist drug war and protect families from displacement. We need stronger tenant protections and an affordable housing trust fund to ensure that future generations have a chance and our family tree isn't cut down because someone with power deems it "diseased."

The Dennison Hotel is demolished to protect the value of the private adjacent surface parking lots.

HOSTILE DESIGN
05/19/2017

Hostile Design is a way to keep people from doing normal things that people would do – like sit, or lay down. These design elements are used throughout the urban landscape to exclude people from private and public spaces. Hostile Design does not include private security forces, CCV cameras, or other elements that require human interaction. But the signs that stand in proxy for security forces can be considered hostile design. Walking through Over-the-Rhine and Downtown Cincinnati, I was able to capture several forms of hostile design.

Outcroppings prevent families and people using wheelchairs from having easy access.

    The most common element that I saw prohibits people from laying down. Whether it be a bench with a bar in the middle, as you see in Washington Park, or it be a circular bench set up, seen in a few places downtown, it's clear that laying down is strictly prohibited. While this may make sense at bus stops, what does it mean when you cannot lay down in a park? Would those people who had a vision for a great city park agree with the mentality to make it as inhospitable as possible? I believe parks were created and designed for a respite from the hustle and bustle of city life. Now, instead of placing the bar in the middle of the bench, they make the benches too short to lay on, such as the bus shelters, including Government Square.

    Another common element stops people from sitting at all. This could be as simple as placing a flower pot on an unused stairway, as seen on 14th Street in Over-the-Rhine, or it could be a slight slope on ledges that would typically be used for sitting. The slight slope makes it impossible to lay down, but it also makes your legs fall asleep if you sit on it for any length of time. Spikes and ridges may be the most shocking type of hostile design, but little fences, such as the one around the entire perimeter of Washington Park are just as offensive. The ridges around the federal courthouse prevent people from sitting on their wall. The ridged metal in front of Holtman's Donuts stops people, who may be waiting on a bus there, from having a comfortable place to sit. The recent removal of many of the bus benches throughout the city highlights the lack of value we put into our public transit system.

Ornate fence around Washington Park prevents sitting or resting.

This is to contrast with the privatization of public spaces, like alleys and sidewalks, in the area. While people on fixed and low incomes are struggling to stand waiting for the bus, a few feet away restaurant outcroppings take up the majority of the sidewalk. People sitting, enjoying their expensive meals can enjoy the sidewalk space, but it is otherwise an offense to sit on the sidewalk. I have seen police officers drive up in their cruisers and tell people they cannot have their legs on the sidewalk, when they were sitting on the church steps. Threats of tickets and even arrest have been made, but restaurants claim several feet of the sidewalk making it very difficult to navigate your way down the street with a family or in a wheelchair, in order to serve alcohol on the sidewalk. These double standards need to stop.

I was first made aware of hostile design several years ago when I was in Santa Cruz, California. The University of California at Santa Cruz was designed to prevent students from engaging in political protests and marches. The winding walkways and meeting spaces were specifically engineered to prevent an uprising. This was done in the wake of student organizing in the 1960's. UC Santa Cruz has become the model for student political suppression and campus design.

Last year, on a trip to Santa Cruz, I was hoping to find something called a "mosquito box." You might be fooled into thinking that a mosquito box would be used to fight mosquitos – a well-known pest. Unfortunately, it is much more nefarious than that. If you've been in gentrifying areas, such as Walnut Hills or Over-the-Rhine, you might be surprised to hear classical music being blasted on the outside of buildings. This is an attempt to push out "undesirable" people from the area. This is also done at Washington Park and the Public Library downtown. I guess the thinking is that people don't want to hear classical music, so they will move somewhere else. This is a type of mosquito box, but not the most egregious.

Washington Park benches, with middle arm rest that prevents lying down.

We have a true mosquito box here in Over-the-Rhine. On the side of Below Zero Lounge, there is a security camera and a mosquito box. Every time you walk by it announces "Warning, you are being videotaped" and gives off a high pitch noise. The high pitch noise is the mosquito box – while it does nothing to repel mosquitos, it causes headaches and forces people to leave the area. Young people are most susceptible to high pitch sounds, so they are more affected by it.

We should consider what it means to be a community and to be inclusive. Does preventing people from laying down solve our housing crisis? Does preventing people from sitting at all give the message that people are "blight" and should not be here? Let's be honest with ourselves – this isn't about preventing crime, this is about our collective denial and our inability to find solutions to hard problems.

WHAT'S IN A NAME?
06/02/2017

Is there a difference between Over-the-Rhine and OTR? Do you use them interchangeably? Do you see them as the same thing? From what I've gathered, many residents in Over-the-Rhine see "OTR" as an affront, as an attempted takeover of all aspects of the neighborhood. Some have even re-rebranded "OTR" to mean "Only The Rich."

When I moved to Over-the-Rhine in 2001, I never heard it called OTR. I was warned of living here, told not to go out at night – even told not to date anyone in Over-the-Rhine because I would get tied up and pistol whipped. I am not even joking. This is the type of hysteria around the neighborhood that even continues to this day – a day when "you are more likely to get hit by a BMW than a stray bullet."

I recently read an article about how developers and land speculators in New York City are rebranding Harlem as SoHa for South Harlem. This is an attempt to entice white people into the neighborhood that is also being quickly gentrified. The act of renaming something should be seen as more than an attempt to "rebrand" but as an act of hostility. When this happens, it's a clear warning of displacement and gentrification.

I remember when the hashtag #ThisIsOTR began to pop up on social media with these professional quality photos on Instagram. To this day, I wonder who puts the pictures up, and what is their angle. Are they trying to promote the neighborhood because they feel that they are a part of it, or do they do it because they want to change the image? Either of these options is problematic, but it is worth considering the effect of the hashtag's prevalence in our social media circles.

Beyond the eponymous "OTR" there are other things that have been renamed here in Over-the-Rhine. When 3CDC began its takeover of the properties in Over-the-Rhine, they began by renaming Vine and 12th Streets "The Gateway Corridor." They put up a big sign where Taste of Belgium is today, and began offering the first set of condos in their newly built Gateway Garage, encompassing the entire block between Jackson and Vine, Central Parkway and 12th. This modern building, with its large fences and gates, sits forebodingly on the main entrance to Over-the-Rhine from downtown. 3CDC has since bought hundreds of properties in Over-the-Rhine, many for a dollar, and they landbank them until they are ready to develop them.

Many of the residents of Pendleton claim their neighborhood as Over-the-Rhine. I have yet to meet a long term (non-white) resident who thought Pendleton is its own neighborhood. So what does it mean when you live in a neighborhood that has a different name than you thought? It shows the level of exclusion that is facilitated by the white gentry.

Finally, one last thing I'd like to address is this exclusion that is constant in the neighborhood. In the past, 3CDC has explicitly excluded people of color from discussions around the takeover of Washington Park. They hold closed-door meetings to make decisions regarding properties that they won't even disclose to the public that they own. But a recent community council meeting drilled into me how disingenuous it is when people call Over-the-Rhine a "diverse" neighborhood.

Diversity is not just the absence of uniformity. Diversity is not just a mix of people. Diversity must include a consideration of the power structures. Looking around at the Over-the-Rhine community council meeting, it is clear that people of color have been directly and systematically excluded from the decision-making in the neighborhood. When there are only a couple of people of color up for election to the 13 member community council board, or that the general meetings have less than 10% people of color attending them, the system is broken. This is not a place to blame people of color for not showing up. This is the time we need to look at how we have and continue to exclude people of color from every plan, step, update, etc. in the neighborhood.

Please do not fall into the trap of gentrification and claim the neighborhood is diverse. Please do not rename the neighborhood as OTR – even if it takes a little longer to say it or type it out. If you want to show that you care about the neighborhood and you care about the long-term tenants, you must resist the glitz and glamour that come with 3CDC's plans, and simultaneously question the self-appointed leadership on their inability to include long-term residents in the planning and implementation of their own displacement.

OF COURSE IT'S NICE
06/30/2017

You know that feeling when you slip into bed with clean sheets and pillow slips? People who are experiencing homelessness aren't afforded that luxury but still try to live as comfortably as possible. The sad thing is, there are many barriers that prevent people from obtaining housing, and many more that keep people from staying in their home. Whether it be a lack of tenant protections, or the fact that we are 40,000+ units short on affordable housing in Hamilton County, it all adds up to a very unstable situation.

Yesterday, I was giving a tour to University of Cincinnati Medical students in hopes of showing them what's happening in the neighborhood, and also giving them an idea of the resources people who are experiencing homelessness have in Over-the-Rhine. Since so many organizations have been forced out by the Impaction Ordinance and developer pressure, a leisurely walk turned into a hike around the southern and northern parts of the neighborhood. As we walked between agencies, I pointed out some of the areas important to community members. In the end, we didn't even make it to Washington Park, because we had to walk so far north to get to the McMicken Health Clinic.

On our way to the clinic, we stopped by the Mary Magdalen Shower House and Ziegler Park. As you may know, the Shower House is getting an upgrade, moving into the St. Anthony building (St. Francis Seraph) where they will have two additional showers for women. We also stopped by the St. Anthony building under construction and talked about the Center for Respite Care, who is moving into there as well. The medical students expressed that they care deeply about the whole person – what are the conditions that lead them to the hospital, and where do they go after they are released? The Center for Respite Care helps people recuperate after visiting the hospital. It must be frustrating for doctors to repeatedly see a patient for preventable illnesses that are exacerbated by homelessness, only to release them to the streets again. This is why the Center for Respite Care is so very important.

For about 4 million dollars of private donations in renovation, the St. Anthony building will house the Franciscan Haircuts for the Heart, The Mary Magdalen House, The Center for Respite Care, a nurse's station, a pantry, a soup kitchen, and a flexible shelter. These agencies perform literal life-saving acts, and it's amazing to see how many people are coming together to make it happen. In contrast, Ziegler Park is getting a 30+ million dollar renovation by our city's preferred developer, 3CDC.

Of course the new park renovations are very nice. While it's not finished yet, the parking garage, pool, and spray ground have opened. While there is some controversy about the pool, regarding memberships, management, etc., that's not my focus right now. Community members without official bathing suits are being forced to tag team bathing suits so that they can at least get some time in the pool. Like at McKee Recreation Center in Northside, we probably could use a swimming suit donation box for the kids in the neighborhood.

The issue with the renovation of the park is similar to the Streetcar – do you think 3CDC wants to spend millions of dollars so that people who are living in poverty can enjoy the changes, or do you think they envision more rich people moving into the neighborhood? It's obvious by their track record of displacement of economic others that these changes are only for the rich. This puts us, low income residents, in a true bind. We too are enticed by the shiny new park, the shiny new streetcars, the shiny new restaurants – but for many of us, the restaurants are economically out of reach ($15 for a hotdog? No thanks!).

Even worse, however, is that the "upgrades" to Ziegler Park have now been documented as a reason landlords are raising rents in the area. Families who are being gentrified out of the neighborhood, are now scrambling to find housing while the Homeless Coalition helps organize the tenants to hopefully save their homes. Every time 3CDC puts a multimillion dollar project in the neighborhood it jeopardizes the housing of people with low incomes. If 3CDC truly cared about people in the neighborhood they would create affordable housing, rather than these half million dollar (and more) condos.

Just a final note on current displacement. I was asked to update on Kroger by an avid reader of *Streetvibes* who was concerned about the Vine Street (Over-the-Rhine) Kroger possibly closing. In an article I wrote a few months ago, I talked about the rumors that the (still non-existent) condos across from Kroger wanted to shut Kroger down because "they didn't want to see people selling drugs out of their windows" in front of Kroger. Even though I contacted Kroger and asked them about the rumors, and they said they had "no plans to close the store at this time," it was recently announced that Kroger will be closing the store in the next two years. In the announcement, Kroger said they have been working on the project for several years – to build a new Kroger grocery downtown. This will double the walking distance for many Over-the-Rhine residents and worse of all, Kroger will be donating the Vine Street store to 3CDC.

Let's not forget who 3CDC is – the board is handpicked by the Mayor. They operate as a member organization, collecting dues from their corporate members – P&G, 5/3 Bank, Macy's, and of course, the Kroger Corporation.

They receive millions in City funding, state tax credits, and other public support. They have bought hundreds of buildings in Over-the-Rhine and they sit on them vacant for years. So what does it mean that one of 3CDC's stated goals on entering Over-the-Rhine was to close all the corner stores – the ones with food and drinks, force us to shop at Kroger, and then close our only grocery store in the neighborhood? This is indirect gentrification.

Privatized pool at Ziegler Park, with rock climbing wall (not pictured).

DONATION STATIONS' SOLUTION CONFLATION
08/11/2017

A week in, and there's still no information to be found on their website. From that, we can only make the assumption that they were woefully unprepared for the project as they tried to rush it out as quickly as possible. But, as we all know, haste makes waste, and now people are confused as to where this money is going to end up.

It wouldn't be so bad except that we are seeing a double standard unfold right in front of our eyes, again. If we were to hold them truly accountable for their work, we would be shocked at how far their intent falls from the reality. Whether it be the loss of public space, the loss of affordable housing, the loss of SRO's (single room occupancy buildings), the loss of Black-owned small businesses, the loss of our identity, 3CDC and its cohorts have demonstrated time and again that they only have one priority, and that's themselves and the wealthy.

I could be talking about a number of their initiatives, but the one I'm fuming about this week (well, one of them, because the pending sale of the library's North Building is certainly enough to make my blood boil) is the parking meters. WAIT! Before you think I'm complaining about parking, you know, participating in Cincinnati's most active sport, I'm actually talking about the "Donation Station" meters that 3CDC, Downtown Cincinnati Incorporated, and the City of Cincinnati have placed in various places in the city.

These meters stick out from the meters you typically see – they are larger and painted yellow. They only take credit cards. The meters are accompanied by a sign:

Donation Station. Funds deposited here go directly to agencies that help our neighbors in need. By using this donation station, you will...
1. Provide food, shelter, and outreach services to our neighbors in need.
2. Fund service providers that help those experiencing unfortunate circumstances like homelessness, addiction, and poverty.
3. Be certain that your money is being used for something positive.

The sign is emboldened with the City's, 3CDC, and DCI's logos as well – using the branding styles of the City and original streetcar design. Finally, a website is given to learn more.

You might be wondering what is wrong with this setup, and you may think

that this is a good thing. What I know, is that this is an intentional step to:
1. Help people feel good about their decisions to ignore people who panhandle.
2. Continue to vilify people who panhandle, by claiming they will use the money for something other than what you would consider "positive."
3. Jumpstart the next round of attempts to further stigmatize and criminalize panhandling.
4. Dehumanize the issues related to poverty and homelessness by mechanizing the point of contact.

There is absolutely no information on the 3CDC website regarding the program. We don't know which organizations will benefit from the parking meters – I mean, Donation Stations. We are seeing a real-life double standard evolve directly in front of our eyes. Each year, almost like clockwork, leaders from the corporate

Donation Station meter on 3CDC's 12th and Vine Street surface lot.

side (3CDC, Downtown Cincinnati Inc., etc.) write op-eds in the Enquirer or get on the news to say that giving to people who are panhandling is actually bad for the people who are receiving the money. They argue that the money is used for drugs, and not for food or shelter. They argue that it would be better to give it to an organization, but specifically to the organization they represent. They demonize people who are struggling in a very difficult time while clearly saying that we don't know where the money will go, just know that it's for bad purposes.

3CDC's website gives us no information as to where this money will go. It doesn't show us that it will go to direct services or to programs. We don't know if it will go to pay for these organizations' half-million dollar per year salaries or if it will actually reduce homelessness. I personally could not take home half a million dollars a year and know that on my watch people are losing their homes, that I had a hand in confirming stereotypes and creating a permanent untouchable class. Just for full disclosure, the Homeless Coalition's entire operating budget is far less than half of the salary of one employee at these other organizations – yet none of them are fighting for an affordable housing trust fund, or no fault eviction policies, or laws that protect people from abuse, or even for a restoration of the human services fund. They convene meetings and talk to stakeholders, yet they never directly address the issue – a lack of affordable housing. In all the work that 3CDC has done, they have not independently created a single unit of affordable housing. The meters do exactly what is intended – to distract you from the solution while stigmatizing the behaviors of those who seek your help.

DOUBLE TROUBLE: DOUBLE STANDARDS
09/22/2017

You probably already know how to recognize double standards when you see them, especially pertaining to things like someone's sex or gender or even race. When a woman is paid less than her male counterpart, that is a double standard. Hopefully, when you recognize a double standard you act or speak out to prevent this oppressive behavior from continuing.

When it comes to homelessness, the double standards don't ever stop. We have a different standard for someone who is housed versus someone who is living without a home. We see this all the time in Over-the-Rhine. 3CDC, Cincinnati Center Development Corporation, which has poured hundreds of millions of our taxpayer dollars into inequitable development (market rate housing and offices), will gladly herald their efforts to close the corner stores that sold beer and liquor in the neighborhood. They will, of course, cite the number of 911 calls to corner stores, then say that by closing them, they have helped remove alcohol from the hands of people who are living in poverty. For them, they see it as a moral choice, and they believe they chose the "right" side.

Woman walks her dog without a leash past sidewalk seating next to Imagination Alley on Vine Street.

The double standard isn't complete by removing the corner liquor stores: this is only half of the standard. The other half is what replaced the liquor stores – high end boutique bars, with more on the way. Loud, beer-laden peddle wagons traversing the streets add to the atmosphere of "we can drink in public, but you can't!" Recently, the neighborhood split into two entertainment districts to accommodate more bars, but from what I heard, one of the last bars from before the surge of gentrification is closing soon, leaving very few vestiges of Over-the-Rhine left. Hopefully, you can recognize the double standard by now.

When it comes to housing, 3CDC is the champion of double standards. When they kicked out the residents on the 1400 block of Race St., they said they were doing the residents a favor because the housing wasn't in good condition. Did they ask the residents what they wanted? No, they just moved them aside for high-end condos and apartments (and their old office, by the way.) The double standard here might not be obvious, but let's look a little deeper and make some historical comparisons.

Man passes Craft Brew sign at privatized Washington Park.

buddy gray, who helped found many social service organizations in Over-the-Rhine, was attacked on many occasions by developers who criticized him for "stockpiling" buildings in the neighborhood. They accused him of keeping the neighborhood poor, and holding development hostage. They lampooned his character and many believe that they eventually assassinated him for this work.

buddy and his collaborators intended for every building to be rehabbed for the people in the neighborhood by allowing the residents to maintain their home here, in Over-the-Rhine. They intended to create and sustain affordable housing. That was the purpose of acquiring the land. And, through Over-the-Rhine Housing Network and ReStoc, they worked with countless people to update and maintain many units of affordable housing – within the last decade, we have lost more than 70% of the lowest income housing units.

Today, 3CDC holds hundreds of properties in their portfolio. They are literally doing the same thing that developers accused buddy and others of doing back in the 80's and 90's. You can't find, nor will they tell, what buildings are owned by 3CDC, because their buildings are registered under LLC's, so as to not let people know who owns them. They have sat on buildings for over a decade without redeveloping them – after they forced, whether directly or indirectly, the residents out onto the streets. Their plan for Over-the-Rhine does not include any independently-created affordable housing. Today, they have 1 or 2 bedroom condominiums for over $250,000.

3CDC also leased Washington Park from the City of Cincinnati for 95 years for $1. They revamped the park by removing people who are experiencing homelessness with 24/7 private security. They have created a park full of hostile design elements like benches you can't lay down on and walls that you can't sit on. They made rules that prohibit laying in the park, giving out food or clothing, or eating out of the garbage cans – all demonstrably aimed at people experiencing homelessness. The double standard here is easy to see as they sell high end liquor and craft beer in the park, but one cannot bring a can of cheap beer into the park. "Buy our beer or else we'll call the cops on you!"

One last double standard is obvious, but you might have just accepted it as normal. This is the cut-outs that bars and restaurants use on the sidewalks. Leaving merely 3 feet of space to pass through, these railed off areas allow bars to serve alcohol on the sidewalks – this is why they must be permanent, to allow alcohol on the sidewalk. So, here we have a privatized sidewalk area where people can drink, but if someone drinks outside of the barricade, especially if they are experiencing homelessness or "not the right class for the new 'OTR'," they may get the police called on them, or at least judged and told that they need to get a job. We must remember that most people who are experiencing homelessness actually have jobs, but the wages are too low and the cost of housing is rising faster than wages.

Whether or not the development is sustainable in Over-the-Rhine is a real concern. But without effort put into creating and sustaining affordable housing, things won't change on the whim of the market. Study after study has shown the need for affordable housing in Cincinnati and we need the big players, like 3CDC, to step up for people in the lowest income brackets. Your bank account does not determine your worth in a just society. Income inequality and housing affordability are real problems, and if we don't get a handle on them quickly, "OTR" will truly only stand for "Only the Rich."

INSTITUTIONAL RACISM STILL LIVES
10/06/2017

After the Great Depression, our government enacted several programs that were designed to increase the wealth and prosperity of the American people. One of the most successful, and financially stable, programs that was created was the Federal Home Administration's (FHA) home ownership program. All the economists knew that if we gave an incentive for people to reinvest in their homes, or create their own single family homes, they could pass that wealth on to their offspring. Owning real estate would create a middle class – which did in fact happen.

The white middle class that exists today is largely, if not fully, due to the FHA program which gave out over 120 billion dollars to people to create single family homes in the suburbs. When we were taught about "white flight" we were taught that it was more of a separatist movement, rather than an economic advantage. But, when we look around Over-the-Rhine and other inner city neighborhoods, and we question "Why are all these buildings vacant?" we have a better answer than "white flight."

The disinvestment of the inner cities was built upon a system that saw African Americans as vermin and proximity to them would reduce the value of property. The term redlining comes from the maps that were drawn in major cities that enabled real estate agents, mortgage lenders, and community leaders to deny home ownership loans to people of color, based upon the collective value seen in their neighborhood.

You have to remember that very few people had any wealth after the Great Depression, so when we think about citizen's ability to pay off any loans, we must recognize that poverty was so widespread that the program needed to be propped up in such a way to ensure success – and this was done by denying loans to people of color, no matter their ability to pay back the loans.

So once again, the wealth of some Americans is dependent on the denial of wealth to other Americans. The system of redlining wasn't just a map with some colors and a rating system – it also included commentary about specific neighborhoods. The maps, made by the Home Owners' Loan Corporation (HOLC), included things like: "Infiltration of: Negroes;" "Respectable people but homes are too near negro area;" "It is 100% poor class Negroes practically all on relief. A high wall, however, prevents their spread;" "Negro district on edge of section, but splendid cooperation of all residents in this section will always prevent spread."

Wholesale denial of these wealth-accumulating loans to people of color resulted in more than 98% of the loans going exclusively to those who were considered "white" at the time. This federal policy, combined with restrictive covenants and Home Ownership Associations (HOA) laws, provided no support or availability of quality housing to people of color – even if they could afford it.

Restrictive covenants were legally binding terms put on the sale of a building – used to prevent the sale of property to people of color. Inside of the deed, whole communities restricted who could buy the property based upon skin color. HOA's had the ability to restrict the sale of the property to white people, and if someone sold their home to a person of color, they would face severe economic punishments (including the absolute loss of the property and fines, imposed by the local court system). HOA's would buy properties if they thought a Black family was interested, just to prevent the sale as well. This created the white middle class at the expense of people of color.

While this disgusting system was officially ended with the Fair Housing Act of 1968, redlining still continues in many ways. In fact, just this year, two local banks (Guardian Savings Bank, and Union Savings Bank) settled a lawsuit out of court which accused them of redlining. These banks only have branches in white majority neighborhoods and charged people different rates depending on their skin color. Both of these banks are locally managed and owned by the same entity.

These types of behavior happen more regularly than you might believe – a few years back 5/3 Bank was in the hot seat for giving people different auto loan rates depending on your skin color. And it happens time and again in other sectors besides housing and loans: education, healthcare, transportation, etc. There is no wonder that Cincinnati ranks 74 out of 77 big cities in America for Black upward mobility – it simply doesn't exist here. This is due to economic factors that crippled the ability of people of color to create and maintain wealth – solely for the benefit of white citizens.

OUT OF SIGHT, OUT OF MIND?
10/20/2017

As I sit here listening to Melissa Mosby, one of the Homeless Coalition's speakers, talk about how people live in their "puffy pink clouds" I am forced to think about how recent actions in Cincinnati are having an effect on people's lives. Melissa says that people don't want to believe that people are experiencing homelessness because it will mess up their version of reality. If they know there's a problem, then maybe they will be forced to do something about it, is essentially what Melissa is getting at. Recent events in Cincinnati make it impossible to not agree with what she is saying.

A couple of weeks ago, our city started destroying the benches that line 3rd Street downtown. On any given night throughout the year, many individuals use the area as a refuge: it's well-lit, close to the Shelterhouse, near bathrooms at Smale Park, close to event spaces that are amenable to panhandling, and there is safety in numbers. In the past, the Homeless Coalition worked for years to get the city to take crimes against people experiencing homelessness more seriously – after years of advocacy, we became the 3rd city in the country to add hate crime legislation to protect people experiencing homelessness. Evidently, these protections aren't enough.

The City Manager claimed that the benches provided an area for people to do all sorts of lewd and dangerous things, but really the call to remove the benches came from Cincinnati Center City Development Corporation (3CDC), Downtown Cincinnati Incorporated (DCI), and other business interests. It did not come from the police or homeless advocates. As we are seeing with the wholesale destruction of the low-income housing in Over-the-Rhine, corporate interests don't include people in poverty, and those experiencing homelessness are seen as vermin who must be removed from sight. Removing us from sight does nothing but create an unsafe situation.

Is it a coincidence that the very week when the benches began to be removed, a woman who was experiencing homelessness was beat to death in an alleyway a few blocks from 3rd Street? Is it possible that this was an attack by someone who simply didn't want to be burdened by someone else's circumstance? It's definitely possible. When we remove people experiencing homelessness from the public view we are putting them in harm's way. I encounter people all the time who stereotype people experiencing homelessness as "dangerous," "criminal," "evil," or "uneducated." These stereotypes are far from the truth, as people living in poverty or homelessness are actually more likely to be victims of crime, rather than perpetrators.

We can readily see this in the youth demographic. Could you guess how many hours will go by before a youth who is experiencing homelessness will be propositioned for sex? Children as young as 9 years old (and younger, actually), are participating in survival sex because they want to have a place to stay tonight. It's within a matter of hours that they will be asked, or forced, into sex with adults. And of course, since drugs are a part of street culture, they will be exposed to, and often forced, into doing drugs. All because they are in the shadows, hiding from their abusers (often this includes their family), they are exploited and abused by people in the streets. This is not a drill, this is happening today. Today in Cincinnati.

The same can be said for adults who are experiencing homelessness that are swept into the shadows. The Cincinnati Police are currently conducting sweeps of underpasses, citing safety and state law. Every time a camp is destroyed and people's belongings seized, we are putting those individuals at greater risk. They are not getting into the shelters because they are already full. Most people are turned away from the shelters in Cincinnati, not because the shelters close their doors, but because they are already over capacity. Sweeping them away like trash doesn't land them in a better situation, it may just land them in a body bag.

THE ALLURE OF GENTRIFICATION
2/9/2018

We get intoxicated when we think about changing the neighborhood. Quite literally, in Over-the-Rhine, we are putting a bar on every corner. But that's not the intoxication I'm talking about. There is a lie, rooted deep within the false narrative of the American Dream, that claims that gentrification is good for a neighborhood. Even the New York Times encouraged its readers this month to visit Cincinnati, and specifically the "gentrifying neighborhood of Over-the-Rhine" as if gentrifying is a good thing, something to behold and embrace. But the reality is much more dangerous than that, and is something we should all be fighting against – here's why.

The biggest issue caused by gentrification is simply displacement. Whether people are displaced from their homes due to rising rents, eviction notices, or the overall loss of housing and small businesses, people are forced to move from their homes under the guise of "cleaning up the neighborhood." Displacement is often done illegally, but because people in poverty can't afford legal council, or don't have the knowledge to fight for their rights, they are left with no way to fight back (unless they work with the Homeless Coalition and Legal Aid to create and sustain tenant organizations.) Displacement also occurs when your neighborhood changes and you are left without the things that made your neighborhood a community: schools, corner stores, social service agencies, public pools, public parks, laundromats, a post office. Why are you in this neighborhood anymore if you cannot afford to go to the new shops, restaurants, or because your family and friends have already been forced out?

Displacement doesn't happen within a bubble – there are many steps that precipitate it, and many of them might be something that you think is harmless, and with which you agree. You might think it's inevitable that the parks become privatized like Washington or Ziegler Park. This issue goes more deeply into neoliberalism, which is essentially the privatization of public goods and resources. Woefully underfunded public goods, like parks, schools, and public housing, become nuisances and "blight" which need an infusion of money to bring back to community standards. The larger picture of "cutting taxes" creates this shortfall of funding, and leaves us with "no choice" but to ask for a public-private partnership. This is what I call "built to fail" in which we know the outcome of underfunding, but we pretend like the people being hurt by it are not worthy of our full investment.

We are seeing this happen at a rapid rate in both housing and public goods. This week, ECOT, an Ohio online charter school, was found to have falsified its attendance records, reaping millions upon millions of tax-payer dollars that should have been going towards education. This is a perfect example of the privatization of public goods because we have now lost this money, and we won't get it back – meanwhile, it will be spent on political campaigns of people who are calling for less taxes (again to underfund our public resources) so that they can grab the next pot of public money – most likely housing. Our public housing is now being converted to private ownership through a process called RAD, which will sell off all of our publicly owned real estate holdings to private companies who will want to make money for their shareholders off of the backs of low-income renters. This is being done in the name of "preserving" housing, but in reality, it is just another way for wealthy people to raid the public coffers.

Other tactics that are used to gentrify a neighborhood include: surveillance, discomfort, criminalization, denial of experience, placing business over residents, forced programming, hostile design, and lack of historical insight. We are seeing each of these tactics occur in Over-the-Rhine right now. Other neighborhoods that are also forcing out residents include Walnut Hills, Corryville, Avondale, Mt. Auburn, Lower Price Hill, and CUF. Each neighborhood has its own community council and CDC (Community Development Corporation) that are making decisions for the community, often without any genuine community input. Over the course of many years, this lack of community input results in the interests of those wanting to make more money trumping the voice of the residents who call their community "home."

A good way to look at this is through the lens of a current issue that was brought to my attention last week: Findlay Playground. The Cincinnati Police Department (CPD) did an assessment on the park, which is located at 5 points – McMicken, Vine, and Findlay Streets in Over-the-Rhine. The larger context of the park is important, as Model Group (and a few other developers) have recently bought all the properties abutting the park, and are turning them into market-rate condos and apartments. The park itself has been underfunded and left to deteriorate. Other parks in the area have been remodeled (yet not privatized), but Findlay Playground's improvements over the past few years have only been to remove things from the park, rather than improve or add.

With the release of the CPD assessment, it is clear that displacement is a big part of the push to gentrify the park. Paradoxically, CPD understands that removing "the criminal element" from one area will just push it to another. In the assessment, they write that "These issues have plagued the area for years and have been exacerbated recently as crime has been displaced from other areas of

Over-the-Rhine." This demonstrates that they are being coerced into creating this assessment by someone with financial interests related to the park, rather than from a holistic view of a community. CPD then calls for most of the park to be removed – the seating, the grills, the basketball court, the picnic tables, the fencing – the people. The claim is that the picnic tables and grills are never used for their intended use: "They are rarely, if ever, used for their intended purpose and mainly serve as magnets for people looking to engage in illegal behavior."

We should be insulted that our community members are being deemed as unworthy to use a picnic table or grill. CPD claims that no one uses the park for legitimate reasons, and essentially calls everyone who uses the park "criminals." Criminalizing people for utilizing public spaces, which might be their only respite in an otherwise increasingly loud and raucous neighborhood, is antithetical to the purpose of a park when your only alternative is paying to sit in a bar.

Surveillance can mean cameras, or it can mean "block watch," or beat patrols for the police, or increased lighting. Surveillance has great implications for the freedom of people who utilize the park and deeper meaning when we consider the "panopticon" and "total institutions" that permeate the loss of freedom and identity in an increasingly policed and imprisoned United States. When our parks, such as Washington and Ziegler Parks, are modeled after prisons, complete with 24/7 private security, dozens of cameras (panopticon), and forced identity, we have to wonder how much freedom is worth losing for so-called security, especially when crime is down throughout the neighborhood.

CPD does not want the park to be comfortable, so they are advocating for the removal of seating and adding a dog park and a workout track. Redefining the use of the park, coupled with more hostile design, which are elements that stop people from doing normal things, such as sitting or laying down (benches with bars in the middle, or are too short to lay down on, bars, slants, flower pots, fences, or spikes to prevent people from sitting on walls, etc.), creates not a park, but a carefully curated area that can only be enjoyed by a select few – those who can often afford the trek to another park.

We are seeing the prioritization of businesses over residents occur at a rapid rate in Over-the-Rhine. Community Council meetings are becoming increasingly hostile to the community member experience, and we are being told that we need to make our meetings more hospitable to businesses seeking entry into the neighborhood. This is coming with a lack of historical insight, both of the wholesale displacement of thousands of units of affordable housing and the longer historical narrative of redlining, racism, and disinvestment which led to the conditions we are dealing with today.

A lack of historical understanding is dangerous, and goes back to the false narrative that the only solution is a market solution. To quote the executive director of the Homeless Coalition, Josh Spring, "There is no market solution to our housing crisis." This is a stern warning that we cannot rely on market forces for solutions in housing, education, parks, etc. as the market is only creating a larger income and wealth disparity, a gap in educational attainment, and a park for the rich and connected and "take-what-you-can-get" attitude for everyone else. Even CPD recognizes the efforts as displacing crime from one area to another – so we need to question where will the crime go next? Innwood Park? Belleview Park? Or should we redefine crime, end the drug war, and engage in racial equity and reparations?

Gentrification is built on the false "meritocracy" narrative of the American Dream – if you work hard, you will be rewarded. We know that this narrative is false because study after study has shown that educational attainment is only linked to family income and spending on curricular materials. We know the meritocracy narrative is false because people born into poverty are not likely to get out of poverty, even if they attend college. We know that the meritocracy narrative is a lie because the rich can do little to no work, yet their wealth increases exponentially. People are getting richer because of gentrification – people are not getting rich from gentrification. No one has been lifted out of poverty because of the development in Over-the-Rhine, yet thousands of people with low-incomes have been displaced from the neighborhood, and at this rate, most middle class people will be pushed out as well. It is only a matter of time.

The CPD Assessment can be accessed online: https://tinyurl.com/findlaypark

MY PICKET LINE
2/23/2018

Last year, my classmates from Walnut Hills High School planned a fun-filled reunion weekend. Even though I have been in Cincinnati most of the time since graduation, there were many classmates that I would love to see. Unfortunately, the planners, with no historical knowledge of the terrible displacement that took place at the Metropole, decided to hold the event at the 21C Hotel. I immediately sent a message letting everyone know how 3CDC unethically and unjustly displaced the residents of the Metropole. I told them that I would not set foot in the 21C Hotel, and I urged others to do the same. It is my picket line.

Growing up in Cincinnati, my first experience with a picket line was when Bigg's employees were on strike. As a child, how could I know the complexity of collective bargaining? But, I was well aware of what's fair and that people should deserve a livable wage and safe working conditions. That instance, of actually seeing people outside a business, holding signs and daring customers to cross the line was instrumental for me in my understanding of labor issues.

Close-up of metal slats preventing people from sitting outside donut shop, at the bus stop on Vine Street.

Recently, you may have seen some of the protests against the new developments, like the Holiday Inn downtown or Richter Phillips Jewelers, which have been accused to be using unfair labor practices. In my mind, I tuck each of those places into a specific space that reminds me not to support that business. I also take the #NFLBoycott very seriously, and I hope that you did the same. I hope you will continue to boycott the NFL in the future, regardless of whether "your team" is doing well, as wage disparity, health/environmental issues, and rampant sexism and racism plague the NFL.

Wage theft is also a huge issue – which means that managers and business owners are withholding pay from their workers. There are many ways in which this occurs, from withholding wages, to pooling tips unfairly, forcing workers to pay back overtime pay, changing time sheets, etc. Wage theft is rarely punished – usually employers receive a slap on the wrist. A recent list of wage-theft businesses was compiled using federal data that included 100 local businesses where the employees have recovered their wages. For example, at the very top, Champion Windows had nearly 700 employees who were finally paid almost $700,000 in overtime that they deserved. Many chain restaurants are on the list, but other smaller businesses, like The Senate in Over-the-Rhine, are also on the list.

In Over-the-Rhine, I listen to stories of residents, including youth, who have received inhospitable service at restaurants, boutiques, or bars in the neighborhood. When someone complains that they were looked over for service, not given water or menus, people seated before them, ignored, poor service, etc., and they believe it has to do with their skin color, I file that business away in my brain as a place I should not support.

Racism and poor labor practices are not the only reasons why I would refuse to patron a business in my neighborhood. Businesses, like Holtman's Donut Shop on Vine Street, where hostile design elements grace their building are also off limits for me. The metal slats under their windows prevent people who are waiting on the bus from sitting down. Even if they just rent the space, they could still do something about it. Businesses that take up a huge amount of sidewalk space with barriers, like Rheinhaus, do that so they can serve alcohol on the sidewalk. Although it is legal, private sale of alcohol is not an acceptable use of public space.

Other businesses are located in places that were key institutions in the neighborhood, like the corner store on 13th and Vine, where Homage is now, or the laundromat where the Mercer is now. I refuse to be a part of the indirect gentrification in the neighborhood. Many other businesses are outside of the price range of myself and the original residents of the neighborhood. We obviously cannot afford to pay the starting dinner price of $38 at these restaurants on Vine Street.

Finally, another trend, using racism/sexism/transphobia/homophobia to sell your product will land you on my banned list. This includes the transphobic half taco, half hotdog menu item from The Senate named after Caitlyn Jenner, or the poorly thought out menu items at Revolution Chicken "honoring" Gandhi and Harriet Tubman. It is very offensive to come into a Black neighborhood, where most of the original businesses have already been forced out, to recreate and rebrand traditional soul food, and make it out of reach of the Black residents through racism, price points, or hostile design.

So the question becomes about how the push for new businesses in Over-the-Rhine actually does more harm than good. Even the non-service businesses offer little-to-nothing to low income residents, like myself, as they carve out private, foreboding, gated-off, areas. I would bet that the picket lines I see in my head are very similar to the places avoided by other low-income residents of Over-the-Rhine. I will stand in solidarity with my neighbors, and I hope you will also do your research and by listening to do the same.

I decided that I wanted to give my classmates an opportunity to see why I envision a picket line at 21C Hotel through a walking tour through Over-the-Rhine. Several of my classmates, who were in town for the reunion, and I met at Washington Park for the walking tour.

FC CINCINNATI: PATERNALISM, GREED, AND RACISM, OH MY!
3/9/2018

The parallels between what has happened in Over-the-Rhine and what is looming for the West End are endless. For those of us who are listening to residents of Over-the-Rhine, who are still being pushed out, we hear the desperation. We know that there is a shortage of more than 40,000 units of affordable housing in Hamilton County, so when someone is forced out, where can they go? This same question should be asked about the residents of the West End.

There have been, and continue to be, meeting after meeting asking for input on the stadium proposal that removes the existing Taft High Stargill Stadium and replaces it with a professional soccer stadium that will accommodate just 20 games in an entire year. But it is clear, no matter how many residents stand up and staunchly oppose the stadium, they will never be heard. FC Cincinnati, the School Board, and City Council have declared, in one way or another, that they will not adhere to the wishes of the community. This demonstrates a clear rift between the community and our elected officials, land speculators, and wealthy businessmen who are thrusting this stadium deal upon us.

Claims have been made by FC Cincinnati that residents just need to be educated, then they will support the stadium. Claims have been made that this will create "good jobs," even though it's not clear how good jobs will come when only 20 games will be held in the stadium each year. Claims have been made that this is the best deal that the neighborhood will ever get, and they should be happy to take it – even if it means being removed from the neighborhood. Claims have been made that a Community Benefits Agreement (CBA) will protect the residents from displacement – but this is an impossibility, a CBA cannot assure us that displacement won't happen. Claims have been made that student life at Taft won't be disrupted, even though there will be a loss of their connected stadium, a huge construction project outside of their classroom windows, and environmental concerns that aren't being addressed.

In sum, the claims that have been made are flimsy at best, harmful to say the least. When I spoke at the School Board's special community meeting, I cited the work I had done in my dissertation – that private/public school partnerships erode student trust, reduce the quality of curricular materials, and chip away at local control of the school. These concerns alone, I claimed, are enough to deny this partnership.

I had listened to the residents, one after another, say they do not want a soccer stadium in the West End, and I was inspired I took the opportunity to call out the racism in the room. The comments by the few supporters of the stadium, all white people, by-the-way, were dripping with racism, thinly veiled micro aggressions, and utter disdain for the people of the West End. I am paraphrasing here, but the audio is available on the School Boards streaming site. "We are throwing our money away when we support failing Taft High School." "I am scared for my safety to speak at meetings in the West End." "Imagine it's 2032 and a girl named Keisha, who got a soccer scholarship to go to UC, is now on the Olympic soccer team."

Beyond the racism and paternalism, we have to realize that we are being duped when FC Cincinnati is running a campaign to take over the neighborhood. By hiring former Cincinnati mayor, Mark Mallory, they are pitting him against his neighbors who, by every measure, strongly oppose this stadium. Even the study commissioned by FC Cincinnati showed that more than twice as many residents oppose the stadium than support it. After a presentation by FC Cincinnati, the NAACP voted to stop the stadium. An unofficial vote at the West End Community Council also voted against the stadium.

Finally, I need to add that the newest tactic that FC Cincinnati is deploying is a logical fallacy in motion – that the residents should fear Citi-Rama more than the stadium. The School Board seems to be buying into this faulty comparison (as one member wrote on Facebook that she believes Citi-Rama, with its high cost homes, will contribute to gentrification more than the stadium) even though the board is not voting on Citi-Rama. The FC Cincinnati stadium will also not contribute to the school tax base. It will not pay its fair share. This alone should be grounds for the rejection of the proposed land swap to build the stadium on public school land.

All of this is happening in the shadow of CMHA's implementation of RAD (Rental Assistance Demonstration Project) which essentially sells all of our publicly owned housing to private developers. CMHA is offering FC Cincinnati the option to buy our land. RAD is bad for our community, as a 5% loss of housing is acceptable in the program. It also reduces resident power. The Homeless Coalition has employed a fulltime organizer to help amplify the concerns of CMHA residents which has resulted in CMHA pushing back – a good sign. Now, let's listen to the residents of the West End, not accuse them of needing to be educated, and stop this stadium proposal once and for all.

EYES ON THE CITY
1/23/2018

How often do you get the opportunity to see your city through someone else's eyes? I have the privilege to do this several times a year through our Cincinnati Urban Experience (CUE) at the Homeless Coalition. Throughout the week, I guide university students through a series of educational and service activities to help them understand how they can get involved in their own community. So far this month, Southern New Hampshire University and University of Vermont have been reflecting on what we've revealed to them about our city. Here are some of the major themes.

1. Cincinnati is racist. From the top down, everyone is impacted by racism in Cincinnati. At City Hall, during the public input session before the Council meeting, person after person got up and talked about the prevalent racism in the Cincinnati Police, which was subject to a recent report by the City Manager, confirming what many of us have known for years — Cincinnati police officers suffer from extreme bias against the Black community. While this could be shocking to some, what was more impactful for me was how almost every speaker also said that the city itself is racist, and that times haven't changed too much for our Black neighbors.

CUE participants, who are here for their Alternative Spring Break, are exposed to many aspects of Cincinnati's racism heritage. From Bucktown to the West End and everything in between, the plight of the African-American in Cincinnati is a direct result of the commonly held racist beliefs in Cincinnati. Our neighborhood, school, and church segregation. Our extermination of Black communities. Our willful participation in redlining. Our refusal to address racism head-on. Our inability to foster a public service that is fair and serves all of the public. These are all markers in our racist city.

2. Collective action is more powerful than following a leader. This lesson is hard to mete out, especially when our history books are filled with individuals who "made a difference," but fail to recognize movements of people who aided those individuals rise out of obscurity. The Civil Rights Movement was not about Rev. Dr. Martin Luther King Jr., Rosa Parks, or Malcolm X — just as the current movement isn't about Rev. Damon Lynch Jr., Iris Roley, or Brian Taylor — it's about the collective power that SNCC, the NAACP, CORE, and other groups did to create systems change. Harriet Tubman did not exist in a vacuum.

So, while leaders come and go, organizations and movements (like the abolitionist movement) need the aid of all people, using all of their talents, and working within specific roles. Black Lives Matter: Cincinnati, the Black Agenda Cincinnati, the Cincinnati Chapter of the NAACP, and the Black United Front, are all strengthened by their members. Organization is how we win. Collective power, such as the determination of many who saved and created the Peaslee Neighborhood Center, is at the core of our future as a city.

3. Voice and Representation are considerably harder to broadcast when your message isn't in-line with a consumerist or capitalistic agenda. Breaking through the lies and myths perpetuated by 3CDC and Cincinnati Mayor, John Cranley, is difficult because the media and 3CDC share board members. 3CDC board members are hand-picked by the Mayor, so there is no representation of low-income, minority people on their board. Just as the SORTA (Metro bus system) board does not contain any bus riders, shouldn't we also be pushing for low-income representation on 3CDC's board? This certainly would be in the best interest of our community, but because 3CDC's goal is to amplify wealth, it would be inconsistent with their culture and values.

Throughout the week, we are honored to have speakers, educational activities, and service opportunities with our member organizations. It's always a pleasure for me to see our member organizations in action and doing what they know how to do best — serve, educate, and advocate. We are lucky to have such great people throughout the city who work at our member organizations and who are willing to share part of their week with us. I want to thank them, but I do hope that they understand the impact their knowledge, wisdom, and experience has on each and every participant. Thank you!

DO YOU SPEAK LIKE A GENTRIFIER?
APRIL 20, 2018

Do you hear things that make your skin crawl? Of course when you hear racial slurs, (including racist mascots and team names), or when you hear someone treated poorly, your ears might perk up and you make note of the words that someone uses. As an educator, it is important to "meet someone where they are" and understand that they may need some clarification or information to make better word choices, because after all, words do matter.

I have written many times about the importance of person-first language when talking about people who are experiencing homelessness. This is to ensure that we don't erase their identities by equating their circumstances with who they are. Person-first language does not diminish the priority of finding housing, but rather operates outside of "deficit culture" which purports weaknesses above strengths. Person-first language also shows that homelessness is a temporary situation, rather than someone's identity. Straight, cis-gender, white men will have trouble understanding this because their viewpoint isn't challenged and they are rarely labeled. This may be where education comes in.

The process of gentrification has many tactics, which result in the displacement of residents. We have begun to write these out in a recent brochure at the Homeless Coalition. Concrete things like tax abatements, community development corporations, neighborhood enhancement programs, surveillance, entrepreneurship programs, dog parks, breweries, sidewalk seating, and hostile design denote the displacement of residents in low-income neighborhoods in favor of increased wealth for some at the expense of others. Interpersonal tactics, such as blight determination, favoring businesses over residents, discomfort, criminalization, denial of experience, and the creation and maintenance of a false narrative, also contribute to the displacement of low income, typically Black, residents.

Under the guise of "cleaning up the neighborhood" tactics are used to both remove low-income and people of color from the neighborhood. The false narrative, that it's dangerous and full of criminals, is constantly used to enable property values to drop so that speculators can gobble them up and wait on them until they are ready to develop for luxury housing. As I have written before, this also happens to our public spaces, including parks. This is more than just a war on values or ideas — this is a war on our community, that some call genocide.

When people call Over-the-Rhine "O-T-R" they are using the language of the gentrifier. When 3CDC (Cincinnati Center City Development

Corporation) began their assault on Over-the-Rhine, they renamed Vine and 12th the "Gateway Quarter," which more than clearly demonstrates their goal. First, to rename it provides an avenue by which they can say "it's not Over-the-Rhine, it's the Gateway Quarter — see, it's safe, and new and shiny!" They attempted to both simultaneously benefit from the gritty, raw, urban landscape, and they allure of wealth. My skin crawls when I hear people call my neighborhood "OTR" as it's the language of the invaders. Even hashtags like #ThisIsOTR were created and maintained by the chamber of commerce, even though they are made to be the voice of the neighborhood. (Rarely do they include people by focusing on street scenes, sunsets, buildings, etc., but that's another story.)

This goes deeper into the development community. 3CDC (Cincinnati Center City Development Corporation) owns hundreds of buildings in the neighborhood now. How many? Well, we don't know. They refuse to release their property list — they told me it's proprietary information. What are they hiding? If you look up properties on the county auditor's site, they are registered under the address, rather than under 3CDC. There are so many LLC's (limited liability corporations) it's impossible to tell which buildings are actually owned by 3CDC. 3CDC will say they are "land banking" but when buddy gray was working with the community to acquire buildings for low-income housing, they were accused of "stockpiling" them. Can you spot the difference between the effect of "land banking" vs "stockpiling?" The language that we use has an effect.

All of this is to say that we all, especially white people, have an obligation to do the emotional labor and to learn by listening to our neighbors, doing research, and ultimately distancing ourselves from people who wish to erase the history, culture, and people from inner-city neighborhoods. We must resist false narratives and lies like "no one has been displaced from Over-the-Rhine," "there are more people living in Over-the-Rhine now than 15 years ago," "more bars will bring opportunity," "a stadium is going to bring jobs," "school life won't be impacted by construction," "it's not removing housing," etc. Just like in everything else in life — if it sounds too good to be true, it most likely is. We must hold our elected officials accountable for the decisions that they make that harm our communities, and we must hold each other accountable when we use hurtful or flagrant language that creates barriers to solutions and the truth.

READ THE WRITING ON THE WALL
7/13/2018

Longtime readers of *Streetvibes* will be quick to point out the lack of "person-first" language in the graffiti: "Kill The Poor!" You may also find offense to the statement as well. When I passed this graffiti, about a block outside of Over-the-Rhine's northern edge, many thoughts swirled through my head: "Who wrote this?" "Is this ironic?" "Are they advocating for violence?" "What's with the quotation marks?" How should I take this statement, on the side of a seemingly abandoned building, on the edge of a rapidly gentrifying neighborhood? What do you make of it?

Graffiti on neglected building reads "Kill the Poor!"

In my mind, "Kill The Poor!" waivers between a rallying call for gentrifiers and a statement of solidarity. On one hand, gentrifiers are using tactics to disempower and displace people who live in poverty and people who are experiencing homelessness. Through over-policing, over-programming of public spaces, raising rents, evictions, privatizing parks, high price points, etc., gentrifiers are gleeful at the removal of "the poor" from private and shared spaces. With a blind eye to history, they believe that if we just remove blight, land values will rise.

On the other hand, those who live in poverty, with little means to invest in the already disinvested community, year after year, generation after generation, see how policy, and structural violence kill them. We see how poor families are separated by the military and prison industrial complex. We see how school districts separate students based upon family income, and how hospital outcomes are determined by zip codes. Even more shocking is that your life span may be dictated by the street you live on.

If "Kill The Poor!" is not a rallying cry, then perhaps, it becomes a statement of solidarity — one that is possibly revealed by the quotation marks. America's war on poverty was inequitable and it didn't seem to lift people out of poverty, but rather created a permanent underclass. The true war on poverty is seen in the cutting of housing options and funding, the loss of healthcare, the loss of affordable education, the loss of civility among the police and fairness in the courts, the loss of clean air, clean water, and clean food. This is the true war on poverty. And it's costing us millions upon millions of dollars — even locally, just in policing and healthcare costs alone. For example, I bet you'd be hard pressed to find someone whose life hasn't been affected by jail or cancer here in Cincinnati. I have to remind myself: it's not like this everywhere.

Small setbacks are major when you are experiencing homelessness. Having a relatively small ticket could lead someone down a path to losing everything very quickly, if they don't have the means to cover the cost. We have seen how evictions cause poverty. This means people will have less money for their child's education, or even food on the table. When our own city can't muster enough political will to spend even 1.5% of our budget on human services, it makes you wonder what our priorities truly are. And, what do those priorities say about us as a city? Are we to assume that people in our city want to help those who are experiencing homelessness, or should we look at how money and energy is allocated to see what we truly value? We must re-examine our institutions.

At times like this, when I'm struggling to gain a deeper understanding of the graffiti within the context of gentrification, I feel the need to challenge my own assumptions. I think of the prolific 20th Century American orator, author, and playwright, James Baldwin, who challenged America to think differently about race and economics. In true James Baldwin fashion, on the 1968 Dick Cavett show, James Baldwin made a powerful statement as a counter-narrative to the idea that he (and the civil rights movement) exaggerates the dangers of American racism.

CHAPTER 3: POWER FACTORS IN THE COMMUNITY

THE SYSTEM IS BROKE (MORALLY)
11/26/2018

At times of reported record corporate profits, record-low unemployment, and high GDP growth, why are we seeing record drug overdoses, suicides, and homelessness? The gap between the rich and the poor is widening, due to wealth and income inequality, to the largest gap in over 100 years. Jails and prisons are overcrowded, convictions are determined by zip code, and prison sentences are extended for trivial reasons so that private prisons keep their determined quota of prisoners. Meanwhile, we are heading towards another housing-prompted recession, unimaginable environmental disasters, and a generation of young people who won't outlive their parents or even pay off their student debts.

There is a common misconception that people experience hardships because they are immoral. To unpack this idea, we need to examine the idea of morality and its relationship to our collective values as Americans. Morality is not determined by someone's religion, although people often confuse these two. Secular humanists are able to understand morality without a text or book that demands certain things from them. Understanding our relationship to others, the ways that we are interconnected and reliant on each other, doesn't require a religious text, it just takes awareness and humility. No one is self-made. No one has accomplished anything on their own because we live in an interconnected system. Even the term "self-made" is an example of capitalist propaganda because no one provided their own birth, their own water, their own electricity, or even their own success, as it is dependent on the comparison to others.

How does this relate to homelessness? For far too long in America the belief that we live in a meritocracy has been both pervasive and disingenuous. The idea that if you work hard you'll get ahead has been proven to be not true time and time again. Janitors, day care providers, home health aides, mothers, asylum-seekers, who toil and strive to work harder each day, fall further behind those who are privileged with generational wealth. No matter how hard someone works in a low-paying job, they will never bring themselves to the level of "wealthy," without the exploitation of the labor of others. The distinction between individual and systemic immorality is a demarcation point for those who possess, and those who lack, compassion.

In Cincinnati, where we have a deep-seated system of pervasive racism, there are morally-lacking individuals who believe that racism is a thing of the past. People actually believe that because there are some successful African-American people in our city that there must be a level playing field. The ignorance of this attitude is not a recent trend, of course, and has been recognized for over a century, with ideas such as the Talented Tenth, as described by W.E.B. DuBois. The idea that because some Black people have been successful *so why aren't others* is a form of victim blaming and gaslighting. Even in that scenario, wealthy Black Americans are subject to unfair lending practices, disparaging remarks, mistreatment by the legal system, and harassment on a daily basis. Racism doesn't stop when your bank account reaches a certain level.

The Homeless Coalition is in a constant struggle to change the system to be more fair, equitable, flexible, and respondent to the needs of people experiencing homelessness, on the edge of homelessness, and our member organizations. We are currently pursuing a legal complaint against the City of Cincinnati and Hamilton County regarding policies enacted this year to remove people experiencing homelessness from the streets and deposit them into jail. Essentially, the legal complaint contends that the City and County colluded to violate the First, Fourth, Fifth, Eighth, and Fourteenth Constitutional Amendments. By refusing to provide adequate facilities for those in need, our City and County have criminalized the actions of people who are just trying to survive. This lawsuit has the potential to affect the lives of thousands in Michigan, Indiana, Kentucky, and Ohio, as we all fall into the same federal district.

With less than 1% of our City's budget going to Human Services, no 24 hour public restrooms, shelters that are above overflow capacity, and a lack of more than 28,000 units of affordable housing, it is cruel and unusual punishment to throw people in jail because they cannot access housing. As I've written before, most people who are experiencing homelessness don't fit the stereotypes that our society has about them. They are striving to maintain a semblance of normalcy, perhaps ashamed about their current condition, and working to hide the realities from others out of fear of judgement, shame, and violence. Essentially, this means that the people who are struggling the most, living on the streets, are being targeted, even though they fit in the same social category as those who are couch surfing, doubled up, living in their cars, or homeless at home. The system's lack of compassion is more glaring and dangerous than anyone's single purported moral failure that led them to homelessness, regardless of the fact that homelessness is a systemic failure, not a personal one.

The answer to the issue of homelessness is not vilifying the individual, but rather from an analysis of our shared cultural values. Some parents have confided in me that they appreciate seeing people who are homeless so they can give their children a "scared straight" message — either do your homework or you'll be "like them on the street." How callous do you need to be to tear others down so that you can build yourself up? What type of modeling is this for your children? How does this extrinsic motivation affect actual outcome, and how does this continue a pattern of "othering" of people experiencing homelessness? Since people of color are more likely to experience homelessness due to historical and contemporary racism, how does this shirk our responsibility to right a system that has had disastrous results for certain groups of people? We cannot value that which we do not understand or care to learn about.

In 2018, with access to information so close to our fingertips, there is no reason that someone should deny that racism exists and affects every person of color. There is no reason that you shouldn't know about redlining, Black codes, Jim Crow, mass incarceration and the preschool to prison pipeline, forced sterilization, unfair medical practices, housing discrimination, inequity, and so forth. It only shows your inability to have compassion, your inability to have morality, and your inability to want better for our entire community. It is lazy for white people to ask people of color to educate us when we are refusing to listen in the first place. It is lazy and immoral.

In the end, it is important for us to decide how we will get involved, and also why. Which torch do you want to carry? Since the 1970's, when federal government spending started to bend towards the wealthy and away from those in need, religious organizations were tasked to pick up the slack of the government. Churches took on the role because it was a natural extension of their stated goals, but it became a way for people to feel better about themselves, rather than changing an unjust system. Even today, sock drives, blessing bag giveaways, water bottles with uplifting messages attached to them, are ways for people with privilege to feel better about income and wealth inequality, rather than having a lasting impact on the community. When you plan to do something, are you more concerned about what you'll get out of it, or what people in need will get out of it? It takes deep introspection to understand that the systemic causes of homelessness (lack of affordable housing, lack of livable wages, and lack of housing protections) are not solved by a clothing drive or food give-away. The problem of homelessness and hunger are only solved by taking the broken system on to ensure that future generations will not experience the same level of discrimination, stereotyping, cruelty, and punishment.

PUSH BACK OR GET PUSHED OUT
12/06/2018

At the last Over-the-Rhine Community Council meeting, representatives from Urban Sites and the Over-the-Rhine Chamber of Commerce came with updates regarding a proposed Service Improvement District (SID) for the southern section of Over-the-Rhine. Downtown currently has a SID that funds Downtown Cincinnati Inc's Downtown Ambassador program to physically clean up the sidewalks of downtown, and they wish to extend this type of program into Over-the-Rhine now that the property tax base has theoretically increased to an amount that could sustain the burden. This type of program can be characterized as a form of neoliberalism, which is not a political ideology as much as an economic ideology.

Ziegler Park's privatized basketball court is now a rental futsal court.

Simply put, neoliberalism can be seen in the privatization of public goods, services, funds, and wealth. We have seen unprecedented neoliberalism in Cincinnati in recent years. From the privatization of the City's Planning Department in 2005 (now returned to the city), to the privatization of The Banks, Fountain Square, Washington Park, and Ziegler Park, there has been a concerted effort to funnel public money into private hands, such as the private non-profit organization 3CDC. 3CDC currently has "preferred developer" status from the City, which basically puts them in front of any line for public land and services.

The designation as "preferred developer" is unclear at best, as there is no formal publicly controlled mechanism for the designation. It may have been the result of a backroom deal, lacking needed transparency. The preferred developer designation makes 3CDC a quasi-governmental organization, and as such, the President and CEO makes more than half a million in compensation each year, dwarfing even the City Manager's or Mayor's salaries.

Findlay Playground fenced off to make way for an income-generating property.

3CDC has been funding sidewalk sweeping for some years in Over-the-Rhine, south of Liberty. According to the representatives, 3CDC has been providing about $250,000 each year to provide this service. They claim that there are 13 workers, who are paid a living wage with benefits. There are several questions to what is considered a living wage, and what benefits are received. 3CDC has stated that this program is no longer sustainable, and the proposed SID would generate $500,000 a year to establish and maintain a new non-profit to run the program. The proposed SID would be a shift of the economic burden from 3CDC to property owners in the neighborhood. Property owners would vote on the SID, not residents. The votes are also weighted, in that they need 60% of the linear footage to vote for the SID for it to pass. Once passed, all property owners would be assessed an additional property tax to pay for the SID. The representative claimed that 3CDC and Urban Sites together own about 30% of the linear footage in the neighborhood, which means their two votes gives them

50% of the votes needed. Adding Over-the-Rhine Community Housing, Model Group, and POAH into the mix, it is unclear how many actual property owners would be needed to pass the SID.

Questions as to whether the SID would increase rent in the neighborhood were downplayed at the meeting by the representatives. They said that it would not increase rents, although they did not provide any research to back up this claim. For those of us who live in "organic" affordable housing, we worry that increased taxes will force our rents to increase. Our landlords don't receive subsidies from the government or promises from 3CDC regarding our tax burden. It is implausible that rents would remain affordable with additional taxes levied on our properties.

Facing pressure, Peaslee Neighborhood Center put "This Building Not for Sale" in their new mural.

Taken alone, the SID seems to be eroding naturally occurring affordable housing. But it needs to be seen in a much larger context. At the same meeting, there was a discussion of the privatization of the alley behind the Transept, on 12th and Elm Streets. At the meeting in October, it was stated that Model Group has purchased the alley behind Findlay Playground so that they can park their personal vehicles on it. Alleyways that have been granted a private lease for 4-5 years by the City have been found to be illegally closed off after their leases, or closed off without a lease by the organization Spring in Our Steps which strives to preserve public alleys and stairways. We are seeing a loss of alleyways in the West End to privatization, including the FC Cincinnati Stadium, which will also permanently close Central Avenue. The Stadium is displacing Taft High School's stadium, many small businesses, a church, and many historic buildings, including the State Theater. This is just the beginning of displacement in the West End, where we are already seeing the loss of affordable housing at the Arts Apartment, and threats to Stanley Rowe Tower.

Facing privatization, youth and community groups fight displacement of community park and garden.

Currently, there is a fight for Findlay Playground, which is located near McMicken on Vine Street. Past privatized parks include Washington Park and Ziegler Park. Washington Park is plastered with advertising from Bud Light, Southwest Airlines, Taft's Ale House, Rhinegeist, 50 West, Christian Moerlein, PNC Bank, UC Health, and CommonBond. The cost to use the park is off the charts, as compared to other Cincinnati Parks. It has private security, with cameras, hostile design throughout, and a liquor license. Results of privatization of Ziegler Park include a swimming pool that went from $4/year to $4/day for the youth. The basketball courts can now be reserved for a fee, and the basketball court is simultaneously a Futsal Court, boasting sponsorship from FC Cincinnati.

A representative from the CRC (Cincinnati Recreation Commission) said their goal is to make Findlay Playground "income generating" which may mean a parking garage, a stage area, or something else. Cincinnati Police have made recommendations to remove all seating, whether official or unintended, and put in a fitness course and dog park. The removal of the play area, grills, and basketball court, according to the police, would help remove people from the park.

Other public initiatives, like the Liberty Street Pedestrian Safety Plan have been put on hold for private interests (FC Cincinnati), which erodes public control of our resources. Millions of public TIF monies that were earmarked for the Liberty Street improvements were transferred to the FC Cincinnati Stadium project. So in addition to the loss of the pedestrian safety improvements, the money was funneled into a private project. On Liberty and Elm sits a vacant field, which for many years was used to grow produce for Findlay Market. Now, as developers fight with residents as to what they can develop there, the field remains empty, and no produce is being grown for the community. There are

Findlay Market gardens, where local produce was grown, vacated for private development.

parallels between these developments and the Main and Schiller development which is threatening a community garden and basketball courts.

Fortunately, community organizations and youth are studying how to do development differently, with a focus on preventing displacement.

Unless there is a concerted effort to fight neoliberalism, we will lose all public spaces, facilities, and services to privatization. Just as there is an effort to privatize the federal Postal Service, there is clearly an increased cost that privatization represents. Whether it be a publicly funded SID, or the use of a park or swimming pool, the cost to use a private facility increases for the user. These costs will ultimately result in higher rents, as we saw when Ziegler Park was updated and nearby residents had their rents raised significantly. The landlord cited the updated park as the reason why the rents were increased. Ultimately, those residents were priced out of the neighborhood and they were forced to move. Who will be next?

KEEP AN EYE ON...
01/07/2019

The new year always brings a renewed interest. People head in droves to the gym for the first, attendance at church spikes, and people's resolutions stay on their mind. In a year, a great deal of things change. This year, we need to be vocal about things that have a disparate impact on people experiencing homelessness, as well as, those who are on the edge of homelessness. The following are a few things that we need to stay on top of this year.

Pricey Policies
For your housing to be considered "affordable," you should be spending no more than 30% of your income on your housing, including utilities. Last year, Duke Energy raised everyone's bill by $200, spread over the course of the year. This rate hike was approved by the Ohio Legislature, and there was literally nothing that we could do to stop it. This year, we are looking at higher food prices, higher cable and internet prices, and higher parking costs. In Over-the-Rhine, south of Liberty, all on-street parking will now be either metered or permit only. The cost to park in Over-the-Rhine has increased dramatically recently, and it is the most expensive outside of the Central Business District. Whether you will be paying at the meter, or for the parking permit, you will be spending more time looking for parking, and more time walking from your parking spot.

   The residential parking program needs to over-sell the spots to be successful. By using my basic math skills, I've found that at full price, the City must sell 1250 parking spots to break even. (There are projected program costs of around $75,000, and the permits cost $60 each. An unlimited number of permits will be sold.) There are only 500 parking spots, so each spot will have been, at least, double sold. The fees and tickets from people who park in the residential parking spots may be able to cover some of the program costs, but what is the psychological effect on people who get parking tickets when visiting the neighborhood? The eventual fall out of this program may force the City to scrap the program, or to extend it north of Liberty. It is a new cost that we all need to keep our eyes on.

Privatization of Public Space
Privatization is a perennial issue that affects us all. In the past, I have written on neoliberalism, and the quest to turn public wealth into private riches. We are seeing a robust movement of privatization in Cincinnati, and across the country,

which is draining our collective wealth in exchange for individual riches. For example, over the past two years, we lost Ziegler Park to 3CDC, who now controls who is able to use the park, when, and how. They provide private security to force people who are experiencing homelessness away from the park. Others have complained that the 3CDC workers have "banned" them from park bathrooms. 3CDC has leased out the park for decades from the City, but they should still maintain their public status. Unfortunately, many people feel that the park is private now.

Brewery District historical trail monuments scattered through the neighborhood, take up a significant part of the sidewalk.

In 2019, we are looking at the privatization of Findlay Playground. Model Group, a large developer, has plans to lease the alleyway next to the park. Last week, I noticed a fence around the alleyway, which to me, confirms that Model was successful with their privatization. Currently, there is a fence around Findlay Playground, and local organizers are trying to collect the stories of those who frequent the park. I have written extensively about how the police and the City team up to create a hostile environment in their quest for gentrification of Over-the-Rhine. Check out the police lights set up around Findlay Playground, watch the increased patrols, and you will clearly see the concerted effort put in place to remove people from the park. This loss of public space continues in other ways as well.

Looking up and down the sidewalk, you will see more restaurants and bars stumbling out into public space. The loss of sidewalk space represents a serious loss of our community. When bars get seating space on the sidewalk, they create a permanent barrier so that people will be allowed to drink alcohol on the sidewalk. While this represents a double standard, as people who are experiencing homelessness are criminalized for the same behavior, it also means that people with disabilities, families with strollers, and large families, are obstructed on the sidewalk. Ultimately, this means that we are pushed out from our usual spaces. Forced to find new routes.

Renaming to Own
The so-called Over-the-Rhine Brewery District plans to have a banner year in 2019. The Brewery District Community Urban Redevelopment Corporation (BDCURC) is getting ready to unveil their own wayfinding signs north of Liberty. You may have already seen medallions in the sidewalk, but have you seen the giant signs that are blocking the sidewalks in some places? The Brewery District's Master Plan's mission clearly shows a lack of inclusion of low-income residents: *"To envision investment and development opportunities for businesses and real estate developers that will be supported by the neighborhood, and that will help guide efforts for physical public improvements to accommodate such development."* By renaming the part of the neighborhood, the Brewery District is trying to remodel the neighborhood into a false vision of the past, which is only inclusive of white, rich, and alcohol guzzling tourists. Look out for other things being renamed, including streets, so-called "Districts," and other public spaces.

Housing Protections and the Affordable Housing Trust Fund
In Ohio, renters have very few protections. Your landlord can refuse taking your rent, then evict you for non-payment of rent. This practice is a threat to stable housing. While change in Ohio may take long, we are looking to push forward housing protections that would stop this type of deceitful practice. Along with the local Affordable Housing Trust Fund, housing protections such as these will ensure people will be able to stay in their homes. Unfortunately, the Trust Fund isn't funded yet, so we will be working this year to ensure funding for affordable housing.

   The Homeless Coalition is currently fighting for the right of self-determination in federal court. If we are successful, we will have prevented the stripping of many Constitutional Amendments, including Freedom of Speech and protections against cruel and unusual punishment and the seizure of personal property. This lawsuit will have a large regional impact, and is definitely something to watch this year.

Special Improvement District (SID)

Another thing to keep your eye on this year is the proposed Special Improvement District (SID) for southern Over-the-Rhine. A SID has existed downtown for a couple decades, which funds Downtown Cincinnati Inc. (DCI). DCI employs people as Downtown Ambassadors who spend the days and night sweeping up the sidewalks and gutters. They are also available for people who have questions. As I have written before, 3CDC, Urban Sites, and the Over-the-Rhine Chamber of Commerce, are planning on hoisting a SID on the southern part of Over-the-Rhine. They are using scare tactics to pressure residents at the Community Council to accept the tax plan. Only 60% of the property owners (based upon the linear footage) need to vote for the SID to impose a tax on all of the properties in the proposed SID. In the end, this will cause rents to raise, and will increase homelessness in our area. It will also create a force to police the streets, pushing people who are experiencing homelessness into the shadows. When SIDs are created, laws criminalizing homelessness are likely to follow. When people are forced into the shadows, they are more likely to be victims of violent crime.

Each of these issues negatively impacts the lives of those who are experiencing homelessness and those who are on the edge of homelessness. Without the efforts of the Homeless Coalition, our member organizations, and our supporters, many of these changes would go by without note, and the voices of those who are affected would be lost.

WHOLLY UNRECOGNIZABLE
02/01/2019

I recently attended a college reunion where a couple of people used the same term to describe Cincinnati today: wholly unrecognizable. I listened to them say that Over-the-Rhine has changed so much that they couldn't even believe it was the same place when we graduated school nearly 20 years ago, in 2001. I heard them talk about restaurants and bars that they uncritically visited while on vacation or with family. I realized then that the optics of the City had changed so much, but nothing else substantial has changed, especially when it comes to poverty, homelessness, and civil rights.

Recent reports put the ethnic diversity of Cincinnati around 1950's United States. We are mostly just Black and white, with a sprinkle of other ethnic identities. And by a sprinkle, I mean less than 5%. African American people are routinely denied healthcare, education, transportation, housing, and other basic necessities. Redlining continues to this day. Schools are more segregated now than ever, as more than half of our schools are 90% (or more) one ethnicity. Most students in public schools (82%) are economically disadvantaged. Home ownership rates among Black families (34%) are less than half of that for white families (74%).

Other objective measures show that Black and white Cincinnatians live in two separate cities. Median household income comparisons show a stark reality: Black median household income at $24,272, compared to white median household income at $57,481. When applied to housing standards of affordability, it becomes clear that Black families are being priced out of their own neighborhoods. For example, a recent developer received preferred developer status on a Vine Street property in Over-the-Rhine through a City RFP process. This developer came to the Over-the-Rhine Community Council meeting in January seeking a letter of approval. Since the Community Council has prioritized affordable housing, the developer claims that 1 of 4 units will be affordable at 60% Area Median Income (AMI). When you take in the great disparity between Black and white resident income, 60% AMI essentially removes any likelihood that a Black person or family would be able to move into this apartment.

I often hear claims that crime has decreased due to investment in Over-the-Rhine and other inner core neighborhoods. But the reality is that crime may actually increase throughout the region due to instability. When people are forced from their neighborhood into other neighborhoods, there are turf issues and issues of representation. According to Census data, at least 25% of all people in Cincinnati moved within the last year, but certainly for some groups this number is higher. Cincinnati crime stats mimic national trends of decreasing incidents of violent crime; however, in 2002 Cincinnati saw 64 murders, and in 2017 there were 70. This is a slight increase, but meaningful when thinking about how things have or haven't changed. Overall, Cincinnati is classified as having more crime than 95% of American cities. Larger looming issues, such as representation in the police force, have remained unchanged. 68.1% of sworn police officers in Cincinnati are white, while the white population in Cincinnati is less than 50%. One police officer as the LGBTQAI liaison. One police officer as the Homelessness liaison. Shouldn't all officers be trained to deal with LGBTQAI and individuals who are experiencing homelessness?

Also deeply concerning is the disparate way African Americans are treated within the criminal legal system. While African Americans only represent 12.5% of Ohio's population, they are 45% of incarcerated Ohioans. While Justice is purportedly Blind, people of color are more likely to be sentenced to death for killing a while person than killing a person of color in Ohio. A white body is seen as infinitely more valuable than a person of color. Your zip code affects your sentencing as well. And neighborhoods in Cincinnati remain so segregated, that our region is #5 in racial segregation. Economic segregation in our region is also near the top of the charts. And your zip code could add, or remove, 20 years to your life expectancy.

In terms of homelessness, we know that systemic and interpersonal racism continue to decrease the housing stability of people of color. African Americans are overrepresented among those experiencing homelessness because of Slavery, Jim Crow, Redlining, Urban Renewal, Mass Incarceration, and Gentrification. Without the generational wealth that white people were handed by the federal government, people of color have no level playing field. Areas that were once deemed "white only" continue to be almost all white. Inner city neighborhoods that were economically neglected since the 1930s, where Black families were forced to live for many generations (because they were legally denied entry to other neighborhoods until the Fair Housing Act in 1968) are now being displaced by white generational wealth. Black families cannot compete with that. African American wealth is predicted to be $0 by 2050, meaning that generational wealth is still exclusively a white policy benefit.

Today, the shelters are still full. We are still short 40,000 units of affordable housing in Hamilton County (28,000 in Cincinnati). While obvious visual changes may have occurred, structurally we are still the same Cincinnati. We continue to criminalize homelessness while privatizing public resources. Our education, transportation, healthcare, public services, etc., are still segregated. Some things have changed: neighborhoods such as Over-the-Rhine, Mt. Auburn, and Walnut Hills have each lost thousands of Black residents since 2001. Between 2000 and 2010 the City of Cincinnati as a whole lost more than 9,000 Black residents. Our neighbors are being forced out by white generational wealth, and we have no mechanism focused on equity. The wealth and income gap between Black and white Cincinnatians has grown, and without a determined focus on affordable housing, living wages, and housing protections, we will continue to see two separate Cincinnatis: one for Black people, and one for white people.

SEGREGATION THEN, SEGREGATION NOW
02/14/2019

The Cincinnati region is home to segregated neighborhoods and schools. The typical American mantra is that we have overcome segregation and with that, we've created a level playing field. Recently, I wrote about how little has changed in Cincinnati over the past couple of decades, and I mentioned that schools are more segregated now than ever, especially when it comes to income segregation. As an educator, I wanted to dig deeper into racial segregation in our schools.

There is considerable educational research that shows that educational success is only linked to two indicators: family income and school expenditures on curricular materials. In Ohio, these two things are intricately linked, as school funding is dependent on property taxes. In a few rare cases, there are some communities who are able to offset their residential property taxes with commercial property taxes, but for the most part, if a neighborhood has expensive homes, the schools in the neighborhood will be able to spend more per student. The school that spends the most in Ohio, spends nearly $40,000 per student on their education. In Hamilton County, Indian Hill spends the most per student; in 2016 that number was nearly $20,000. These amounts dwarf the $10,000 spent on each student in Cincinnati Public Schools.

As my work brings me in and out of schools on a constant basis, I am always surprised when I visit a non-segregated school. It is rare, but it does happen. I wondered what this would look like, on a statistical level, so I began doing a data search. The State of Ohio keeps records on public schools, but does not provide information on charter, private, or religious schools. Since the segregation in the Catholic Schools in Cincinnati seems to be anecdotally related to racism: as my family members have vocally said they will send their children to Catholic schools because there are "too many Black people" in the public schools, I can readily and wholeheartedly say that the push for a Catholic school education comes more out of racism than their adherence to Catholic beliefs. However, the Catholic schools in Cincinnati aren't completely white, as many schools are completely Black, especially at the elementary level. An example of this is in East Walnut Hills, where St. Francis de Sales Elementary is almost entirely African American, and Mercy Montessori, just a few blocks away is mostly white. Until the demographic information is made available, we can just go from our experience, and know the Black Catholic schools and the white Catholic schools.

Focusing on the public schools has the benefit of also thinking deeper into the racial dynamics of the neighborhood, or municipality, in which the schools operate. In my research, I am including the demographic data from 49 local schools. I was unable to get Ohio data from Dater, Gamble, Taft, and Seven Hills School, which I suspect are each racially segregated. I also had to use Mason Middle School data, as the high school data wasn't on the state's page. Finally, Harrison High School data was not available. However, the data I did collect represents more than 50,000 students in the Cincinnati region, in Ohio. I did not include Northern Kentucky, although recent reports put that region near the top of the most economically segregated schools in America. When school desegregation efforts were in full swing in the 1970's, the definition of segregation was a school with 70% or more of one race or ethnic group. This is the standard that I am using here. The results below show that most students in Cincinnati go to a segregated school.

The level of segregation would be shocking, if we didn't expect this to be the case. Of the 50,274 students in the 49 local schools, 34,814 students attended racially segregated schools. Far more than half of the attendees. 9 schools have less than 10 African American students in attendance: Ross, Claremont-Eastern, Bethel-Tate, New Richmond, Goshen, Taylor, Mariemont, Batavia, and Madeira. The total population of these schools is 5,237 students. Less than 90 students total, in all of these schools, are African American. Ross High School has the distinct honor of the most white, at 98%. Other schools that are 90% or more white include: Amelia, Loveland, Turpin, Anderson, Oak Hills, Milford, and Little Miami Local School District. Schools in the 80-89% white category include Lebanon, Kings, Reading, Monroe, and Indian Hill. Schools that are 70-79% white include: Wyoming, Lakota, Deer Park, and Norwood. This leaves Sycamore on the border at 67% with an 8% African American population.

It should be noted, that these levels of segregation are not natural, and that segregation comes from decades of racism in housing, education, employment, transportation, health care, etc. None of this "just happens" but rather it is a concerted effort by banks, real estate professionals, racist policies, and policing. Many of these communities were "Whites Only" communities, through redlining, restrictive covenants, and other concerted efforts to exclude people of color from settling there. This is also not some historical issue, if it was, then we wouldn't continue to have severely segregated schools.

There's another side to this, where schools are segregated at more than 70% African American. The most segregated Black school is Woodward, (again Taft data wasn't available, which I suspect is very highly segregated as well), with 94% African American, and 1% white. Shroder comes in second at 93% African American, followed by Hughes at 90%, Aiken at 86%, Withrow at 83%, North

College Hill at 81%, Western Hills at 78%, Mount Healthy at 74%, and Virtual High at 70% African American. Other than North College Hill and Mount Healthy, these are Cincinnati Public Schools. Generational poverty creates a more expensive remedy for these schools, as schools are forced to pick up more slack, even serving two or three meals a day, ramping up wrap-around services such as medical care, and providing family-based education options. In general, schools that are majority white have less additional expenses because of the generational wealth that our public policies granted them over the last generations.

There are some schools that aren't so severely segregated, but I might argue are still segregated, but they have a larger Hispanic or Asian population, which tilts the numbers into 3 boxes, instead of two: African American and white. This includes Princeton, which is 23% white, 46% African American, and 21% Hispanic. While no one is a majority alone, it reaches segregation levels while including Asian and Pacific Islander as well. Also, I would put Mason City Schools into this category as well, with 61% white, but less than 4% African American. There is a large Asian population in Mason schools, at 24% of the student body. Winton Woods also fits in this category with 27% of the students of Hispanic, Asian, or multiracial identity. A discussion about the so-called "model minority" in education, what that means for other minorities, and how this dilutes race-based measures, will need to be saved for another article, but it's an important consideration when looking at the statistics.

We are left with 11,120 students who attend desegregated schools, based upon the formula I discussed above (70% threshold). Each of the following 10 schools have less than 70% of a single race or minority grouping. The percentage of African American and white students total in each school is between 80 and 88 percent. While these numbers may not accurately portray the community within which the school resides, as there are other schools, such as charter and religious schools, it may make a statement about the school's commitment to creating a social system that enables students to make informed decisions on their exposure to people of different ethnicities. Four of the schools. Clark Montessori, Oyler, SCPA, and Walnut Hills are Cincinnati public schools, while the other six are mostly suburban schools: Colerain, Fairfield, Finneytown, Lockland, Northwest, and St. Bernard/Elmwood Place. Only one school, SCPA is more than 50% African American, at 53%.

These numbers don't get to deeper issues of representation. What does it matter if a school's student population is desegregated if there are no African American teachers or administrators? How are Black students treated differently when it comes to punishments, or even advanced courses such as AP? What is the graduation rate for African American students? What is the level of police presence in each school? How are the relationships different between students and staff, including detention guards and so-called School Resource Officers? But what we can gleam from this data is that we are still in an active mode of segregation when the vast majority of our students attend extremely segregated schools, live in segregated neighborhoods, and ultimately, live segregated lives.

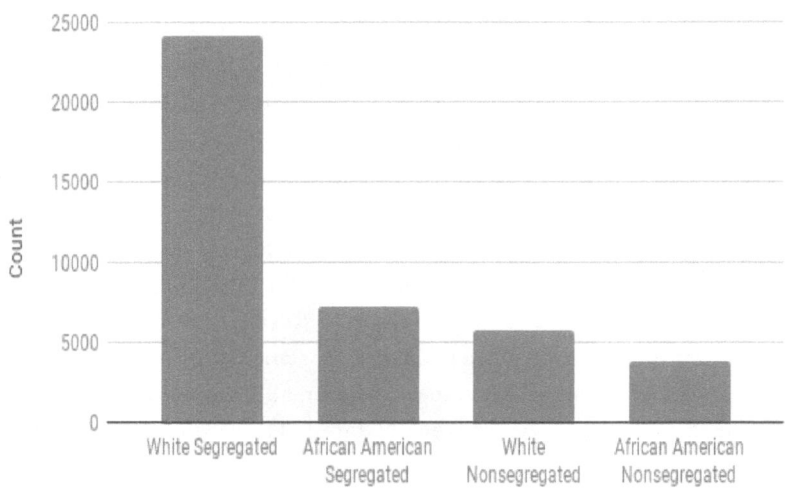

Students by Race and School Classification.

DISAPPEARING COMMUNITIES
03/27/2019

Over the years, Over-the-Rhine has been changed by outside forces. People who live in the rich, white neighborhoods, have come into our small neighborhood and stood for one thing: displacement. Their explicit goals: to displace corner stores, to displace crime, to displace our institutions, to supplant their version of public goods onto our assets. We have lost so many of our neighbors over the last few years, that we know at least 2,400 units of housing have been lost to gentrification, never to return.

But let's not confuse progress with the status quo. As I've written before, the changes happening in Over-the-Rhine are not progress, as they are just the wealthy making decisions for everyone who has less resources. This is not progress. This is the status quo.

The Cincinnati Recreation Commission has been at the center of many of the losses we have succumbed to in the neighborhood. The loss of our public pool at Ziegler Park, the potential loss of Imagination Alley, the potential loss of Findlay Playground. There has been a makeshift fence around Findlay Playground for months now – displacing the normal patterns of residents who utilized the park for years, perhaps even decades. The alley, Goose Alley, which borders Findlay Playground has been sold or leased to private owners on the west side of the alley. This prevents the public from taking in the murals that are along the wall there – a public art project that many will never get to enjoy, due to privatization.

Larger questions of ownership of Findlay Playground have been discussed in my articles before, but it brings into the light how vulnerable our public assets are due to gentrification. It's easy to understand gentrification if you understand the word displacement. Gentrification is displacement. The story of Over-the-Rhine goes back a long time, and it wasn't some sort of German utopia – even if that's what current developers claim as they fetishize our history. The ancestors of the Adena, Hopewell, Osage, and other Native Americans were killed and pushed back by the colonizers who arrived at the Ohio river shore. They were displaced, yet their story is never considered as part of the history of Cincinnati.

The displacement that is occurring today is the fall-out from the Great Depression, and the federal policies that resulted from the depression. The Federal Government desired to create social economic policies to uplift the populace out of poverty. However well intended, African American people were systematically cut out from that plan. Moreover, African Americans were labeled "vermin" by the same government that is meant to represent them. The Home Owners' Loan Act (HOLA) was part of the New Deal, and it prioritized white people and communities over people of color. It is regarded as one of the greatest tools that created generational wealth that white families have today. Black people were denied participation in the program, so much so, that over 98% of the loans went to white people. Black people, even if they could participate economically, had the door shut in their faces. Today, the wealth gap persists between Black and white communities, largely because of the discrimination that was legal at the time, (yet still persists today.)

What does this have to do with Findlay Playground? Well, following the money available, approximately 120 billion dollars (1930-1970 dollars), the white people who participated in HOLA, used the federal money to create white-only communities, which we affectionately call the "suburbs" today. Racial segregation policies, such as restrictive covenants and straight up "Whites Only" ordinances, were not found to be unfair until 1968, after the HOLA program ceased giving out the low interest, fixed rate, mortgages. White wealth was created through home ownership, and Black families were shut out of both the opportunity to participate in HOLA through redlining, and they were shut out from communities of wealth through legally supported racist housing policies. So what were their options?

Black families were forced to live in areas centrally located to the cities, which have seen the most disinvestment and the most loss of wealth. From the 1960's to the early 2000's, these inner city neighborhoods were vilified, strangled by disinvestment, and told to pull themselves up by their bootstraps. Meanwhile, the federal government infiltrated movements to improve the conditions in Black neighborhoods, while simultaneously destroying them with an influx of illicit drugs and the eve of mass incarceration. The police continued their legacy from the "slave catching" days and separated as many families as possible to create chaos in Black communities. So, what do Black communities have left, when the City has abandoned them, the wealthy whites have created their own separatist communities, and the grip of racism keeps them from getting "out of poverty" even though they do all the things that they are told to do? Cincinnati still has no possibility of upward mobility for African American residents to this day.

Our only assets then, besides our neighbors, are our public assets. Most of the buildings in Over-the-Rhine are massive, owned by out-of-state landlords, or local white people, who are out to make a buck. Fortunately, the Over-the-Rhine Peoples' Movement was able to acquire buildings, because without those, we would have very little control over housing in Over-the-Rhine. But, for the most part, the only assets that we share together are our parks, our playgrounds, our schools, our sidewalks, alleys, streets. 3CDC took aim at each of these public assets and has worked to privatize them and force out the existing residents for new, whiter, wealthier, ones. This has been totally at the expense of low-income Black residents and moderate to low income white residents, who enjoyed the first wave of gentrification and are now being forced out for the next wave of wealthier white people with generational wealth.

Today, the police have become such a fixture in our neighborhood, that it's not uncommon seeing them driving the wrong way up Republic Street, or sneaking around corners in their cruisers, creating an atmosphere of distrust and hostility. The main role of the police is to split families up, not keep them together. The main role of 3CDC is to displace poverty to another location, not uplift people out of poverty. The main role of the CRC should be recreation, but it's becoming more clear that their bottom line is a financial consideration. So, as they strive to make Findlay Playground "income generating" they are literally siding with the wealthy over our neighbors who find themselves being squeezed out of their own neighborhood by generational white wealth.

I wonder if the Director of the CRC, who is making the decisions behind the sale and lease of our public lands, knows the specific history of Over-the-Rhine. I wonder if he understands the important role of public assets and the current attack upon them. I believe that if he understood the pain and anguish that we experience when we lose our public spaces, that he would work harder to defend them, rather than look at them as ways to make money. The CRC Director is not a Cincinnati native, which follows the trend of hiring outside of our own community. His view of Cincinnati started in 2016 when he arrived to start as the Director of Recreation. His understanding is not the same as someone who grew up "Down da Way," and who spent their youth on the basketball courts that have been lost now. He doesn't see the city from our perspective, and his interactions at our community council meetings show that he is only concerned about the almighty dollar, not about the enrichment of the youth and community who are the true owners of the public assets on which he sits. His position is not one from unencumbered racism and class warfare. Cincinnati has a specific history, which didn't start, nor end, with the German immigrants, but which is a rich cultural tapestry of many immigrants and migrants who deserve to access our public assets.

HOW TO BURY A STORY
04/11/2019

The old adage in news broadcasting, "if it bleeds, it leads," helps create the belief that the world is more dangerous than it really is. Violent crime is at its lowest point in generations, yet people still believe that the world is more dangerous today than ever before. While mass shootings have become commonplace, the likelihood that a random act of violence will affect you are slim to none. The vast majority of crime occurs between people who are connected in some way. Rape and molestation are more common among family members, acquaintances, friends, and social groups than the random person on the street. Yet, we start early with "stranger danger" which may lull children into the false belief that their family and friend group are safe from harming them. Our limited, and perhaps distorted, worldview can be more harmful when we believe falsehoods touted by media.

Currently, community groups, including the Homeless Coalition, are in a media battle surrounding residential displacement in the West End. The soccer company, FC Cincinnati, has bought several buildings in the West End, and they are currently trying to remove the long-term residents, including 99 year-old Ms. Mary Page. The optics on this are pretty astounding, as Ms. Mary is bedridden and seeing her, hearing her story, is compelling. Yet, local news media are attempting to bury the story to protect the wealthy elite who own the soccer business. This is the type of story that should be running nationwide by now, yet, it is barely making rounds on local news sites. While Ms. Mary is just one of many, (FC Cincinnati's own housing study, to be released the summer, shows that more than half of the residents of the West End, not including public housing, are at risk of losing their homes in the next 3-5 years), the stress of displacement may not just result in homelessness, it could also end her life.

One of the ways corporate media tries to bury the story is through oversimplification. Media may try to frame things as only two sides, and that each side has only their own interests at heart. In the case of the soccer stadium, it is presented as the soccer stadium is just trying to be built, you know, for economic development, or progress. This viewpoint does not take in the months of organizing against the stadium, the residents who almost unanimously tried to stop the stadium from coming to their community, the land-swap deal with Cincinnati Public Schools, the many variances and zoning changes that were brought to City Council, research that shows that stadiums are economic wastes, and the whole history of the Bengals' stadium deal – which we are still paying for in the county. Trying to simplify the issues also leads to a forgone conclusion, such as we saw in the news this week, which claimed that the residents must move for the stadium. Not only does this ignore the promises made by Jeff Berding of FC Cincinnati to "not displace anyone" it also defies logic – they do not need to move, but the business interests don't value their lives because they are not in the targeted demographic for the stadium or the newspaper.

Another typical tactic used to bury a story is to discredit the sources, those who are affected, and those who are helping to organize and amplify voices. Discrediting is seen in the titles assigned to people involved: community leader becomes "activist;" community organizer becomes "advocate;" community member becomes "bystander." We see this time and time again, and it's written into the history as well. Somehow, without having political aspirations at all, we at the Homeless Coalition are accused of staging the fight against displacement "for political gain." I have yet to figure out what that gain is. How do we gain politically when we are aligning ourselves with the people who are thought to have the least amount of power? If we wanted political gain, wouldn't we align ourselves with the most powerful? This kind of logical fallacy is prevalent in the media as it attempts to discredit the hard work that organizing entails. Other ways that sources have been discredited this week, include statements regarding Ms. Mary's caregiver and family member, who lives in Mt. Auburn, that claim that she's not worried about losing her own housing. What does that have to do with this issue? Unless we are talking about multi-neighborhood gentrification, it's irrelevant. We should all be worried about displacement, and it should not be down-played by the media. But the goal here was to say that it doesn't really affect the caregiver, so why is she even speaking about it?

Even more egregious than the previous examples, is when the news media clearly side with the oppressor, or agitator. In the case with FC Cincinnati, media outlets were quick to cite false information provided by FC Cincinnati, including that they were working directly with Ms. Mary (and others) to help them through this transition. FC Cincinnati was attempting to hide their new ownership of the buildings, and they were not at all in contact with the residents being displaced, other than notices to vacate the building. By repeating lies over and over, that FC Cincinnati is being altruistic, trying to help, when they have not even had a phone call or meeting with the residents, is a clear example of bad journalism. But beyond bad journalism, or what might be called fake news, it also shows how eager the media is to take what the powerful and wealthy have to say and run with it. It should have never been in print without verifying the facts. There have been other false statements made by FC Cincinnati over the years, including that no one would be displaced, and without a critical media to analyze these false messages, we are left with a mouthpiece for the soccer business.

Distracting the reader/viewer is also done to ensure that the whole picture isn't received. A promotional video for the proposed soccer stadium ran on top of a recent article about the community members who FC Cincinnati is attempting to displace from their homes. The video, with its upbeat and driven music, shows fancy sketches of the possible stadium, comparisons with existing buildings in the area, including the football stadium, and glamorizes the stadium site. The video itself is overpowering, and I even watched the video thinking it was going to be about the victims, but it turned out to be a promotional video provided by FC Cincinnati. I watched the entire video before realizing that it didn't even relate to the content of the article. The video itself is so hype that I was exhausted after watching it and I didn't even read the article. Hours later, after realizing that I missed the content, I had to go back to the news site, skip the video, and read the article. To distract us from tragic displacement, I also noticed non-story news popping on the front page of corporate media sites. For example, stories about the 7 Hills student who died in his van last year, and failures of the 9-1-1 system somehow became news again. Lists of hole-in-the-wall restaurants started popping up on corporate media's social media. The story will be buried through distraction and oversaturation of non-news. Sports plays a specific role in distracting the public from inequalities and inequities that negatively affect our community's quality of life.

Finally, the use of logical fallacies is prevalent in the reporting around the displacement of the low-income, mostly Black, residents in the West End. An Operation Vortex style blitz is being touted by the Cincinnati Police Department as a solution to the crime of the West End. These types of activities only serve to displace crime to another part of the city. The notion that everyone in the community is a criminal is not only harmful, but serves specific interests, including that of FC Cincinnati and land speculators. When social media pointed this out last year, the Cincinnati Police Department fired back by claiming this is what they do every year. So, every year, they label an entire neighborhood as criminal and become aggressive with them. Does anyone else see this as a problem?

We cannot simply compare FC Cincinnati, with its unlimited monetary resources, with the low-income community it is attempting to control. These are not equal comparisons, and should not be treated as such. We should be mindful of the tactics used to bury the story: oversimplification, forgone conclusions, discredit and deny, siding with the oppressor, distracting the community, using promotional materials as news, using blanket statements that vilify entire communities, and pretending that the villain and the victim have the same amount of power. Like rape and sexual assault, the attempt by FC Cincinnati and its corporate partners to take the West End for their own use, is about power and control. FC Cincinnati, with the blessing of Cincinnati Public Schools, Cincinnati City Council, and the Hamilton County Commissioners has the power to do many things, but they cannot erase the power of the people who are organized and unified with a single demand: to remain in their safe and affordable housing, ultimately, to not be removed from their own community.

AFFORDABLE FOR WHAT?
5/16/2019

We are in the middle of an affordable housing crisis. The crisis is not just in Cincinnati but it is widespread throughout Hamilton County and the region. With over 40,000 units of affordable housing missing in Hamilton County alone, we are facing an unprecedented housing challenge. They're many different ways to calculate whether or not someone is paying too much for their housing, but commonly we believe that if you pay more than 30% of your income towards your housing, you are then paying too much and are rent burdened. When families are rent burdened, they are just one paycheck away from a crisis that can negatively impact their lives.

In Cincinnati, we have many different organizations that are fighting to make sure that we have affordable housing available to all, but they haven't stopped the free market from creating a very difficult situation for many families. We are fortunate in Over-the-Rhine to have organizations that are ensuring that some families are able to remain in the neighborhood. Unfortunately, over the past 15 years, we have lost more than 2,400 units of low income affordable housing in our neighborhood alone. Organizations like Over-the-Rhine Community Housing enable us to not only sustain units of affordable housing but also bring new units online. Over-the-Rhine Community Housing has been partnering with other organizations, like Tender Mercies and Community Matters, to create new housing in Over-the-Rhine, the West End, and Lower Price Hill. Tender Mercies works with adults with developmental disabilities (and histories of homelessness) to ensure that the most vulnerable in our community have stable housing. They use a "housing first" model to get people into housing while they deal with mental illness or addiction. Tender Mercies has a couple of buildings on 12th Street, and a few more throughout the neighborhood. They have been a model for SRO housing (single room occupancy housing) throughout the region and perhaps the country.

Tender Mercies and Over-the-Rhine Community Housing have partnered on new housing in the West End. This new building, on Ezzard Charles, will provide housing for people who are today housing insecure. Combined with the nearly 500 units of affordable housing that Over-the-Rhine Community Housing provide, we are lucky to have such a comprehensive organization in the neighborhood. Over-the-Rhine Community Housing not only provides affordable units of housing, but it also runs the Jimmy Heath House and the Recovery Hotel. The Recovery Hotel gives people a chance to get through drug and homelessness recovery while not giving them a time limit to do so. The Jimmy Heath House provides wrap-around services, such as social workers, to make sure that people will be successful in recovery and out of homelessness. The Jimmy Heath House also houses the employment pipeline, which gives people an opportunity to work toward full-time employment at several local organizations including Nehemiah Manufacturing, Building Value, and the City's Parks Department.

A No Trespassing sign greets visitors to Imagination Alley.

Another organization in the community that provides affordable housing is the Preservation of Affordable Housing, or POAH, which has taken over many of the formerly Brickstone properties. Brickstone was a part of the developer Model Group. Brickstone was known for creating and sustaining high quality affordable housing throughout the city. Many Brickstone buildings are scattered throughout Over-the-Rhine, Mount Auburn, and other surrounding neighborhoods, including Walnut Hills and Avondale. POAH manages Brickstone and some Model Group buildings. One of the buildings that Model Group owns and POAH is the manager, is Parkway Towers. Parkway Towers has been a building for older adults and people with disabilities for many years. Over the last few years, there have been some changes at Parkway Towers, which have been concerning to the residents. Not only has management changed, but also ownership. Residents are now being forced to leave the building for a renovation to widen the hallways. The Parkway Towers' tenant organization has been negotiating through the whole process. They have created a survey of the residents to ensure that the people who are most vulnerable will be able to return to the building. This process started with a 45 day notice for residents to vacate a couple of years ago, but with the organizing of the tenants, and with Legal Aid and the Homeless Coalition, they've been able to remain in their home so far. Other organizations in the neighborhood, that help create and sustain affordable housing, are very limited. There is some organically occurring affordable housing in Over-the-Rhine, but much of it is disappearing very quickly.

The way to calculate whether or not you are paying too much, is by taking 30% of your gross pay and applying that to your housing, including your utilities. There is also a nationally recognized fair market value for one, two, and three-bedroom apartments. The fair market value is determined by the cost of living in any given area. For our area, a one-bedroom at fair market value is about $645 per month. The amount for a two-bedroom apartment is about $800 per month. And the fair market value for a three-bedroom apartment is a little bit more than $1,100 per month. This fair market value is essentially what the federal government would pay if you were receiving a subsidy for your housing. Certain governmental programs will pay approximately 120% of the fair market value for a unit. Those who receive these subsidies might be receiving a Section 8 voucher, where they are able to find housing in the private market. Other people might be receiving a subsidy through the organization that owns the building or on their own. Many years ago, the federal government decided to move away from project-based housing and into the subsidy of private units. The idea was deconcentrate poverty, but little data has shown that this effect has been positive for the community. To look at it from another perspective, think about the concentration of wealth in certain neighborhoods in our community, and consider whether or not low-income subsidized housing would be welcome in that community. Chances are pretty high that that community of concentrated wealth would work hard to block low-income affordable subsidized housing in their community. So whether or not poverty has been deconcentrated is still up to further research. We do know that concentration of wealth has created barriers between communities who are in need and those who are able to facilitate those needs. Ultimately, however, it is the responsibility of our government to make sure that people have safe and affordable housing.

Fortunately, in Cincinnati, we have an organization called Affordable Housing Advocates, who is advocating for affordable housing throughout our region. But when it comes down to it, housing is always a question of affordability. When a low-income unit is taken offline, chances are it will never return. Without advocates working day and night throughout the year to create more affordable housing, we will never chip away at our 40,000 units shortage of affordable housing. While organizations listed above are doing housing work to ensure that affordable housing is available, each one of these organizations has a waiting list that means that people can take months, to even years, to get safe and affordable housing. This is a structural issue that needs a systemic solution through local, state, and federal governments. The market will not solve this problem, so a reliance on the market will only make the issues worse, and affordable housing will be even more difficult to obtain.

PARTICIPATORY BUDGET
6/27/2019

When you look around your neighborhood, what do you see? Do you focus on the people, going on about their day? How about the buildings and the businesses in them? We rarely take time to look deeply at the publicly owned assets that make up our community, but when they are in disrepair, we notice that someone needs to do something about it. But, who? And when?

Look closely, a streetcar pole retrofit into a utility pole, with a piece of wood placed on the top for private electric lines.

I want to feature the four or so blocks between Liberty and McMicken on Vine Street. The Vine Street Corridor is known as the main street between the east and west sides of the city. As Vine Street snakes its way up from the urban basin, it passes main institutions, such as the University of Cincinnati, the hospitals, the Zoo, churches, schools, and parks. Of course, many neighborhoods and housing is also located on, or near, Vine Street. I don't know the exact origin of the name "Vine" for the street, but my theory is that it was named Vine Street because of Longworth's hillside vineyard that spanned the hillside from Fairview to Reading Road. Therefore, a trip up Vine Street would bring you to the Vineyard before anything was built beyond the hillside.

Local governments who struggle to fund simple (and necessary) things like sidewalks, sewers, utility poles, and lighting, while at the same time finding funding for millionaire pet projects, should be ashamed of themselves. On this stretch of Vine Street, which is the most important street in our entire city, you can feel the shame of disinvestment. Broken sidewalks, crumbing curbs, rusty lights, and bootleg utility poles, all line Vine Street between Liberty and McMicken. A crumbling infrastructure greets the residents of this stretch when they walk out of their doors each day. The amount of pride someone takes in their neighborhood is probably affected by disinvestment like this. Yet, residents are blamed for not taking care of the neighborhood when litter is visible, or graffiti covers a wall. So many of the buildings are boarded up, yet many families are raising their kids along this corridor.

A participatory budget is a type of governmental public input process. Essentially, when residents get to have input on the city's budget, the values of the people are expressed. Our current budget process could be described as a "sham" because it is all about political posturing. The City Manager proposes a budget that outrages everyone just so the Mayor can come in and "save the day." The community input sessions are shameful displays of inhumanity as people have to argue not to have their projects or positions put on the chopping block. The sessions generally last hours, with only some City Councilmembers in attendance. It's important for people to show up, but it all just seems like political theatre to me. What if we started with the budget of the people, and then approved slight modifications from politicians? Do you think we would give the majority of our budget to the police? Or do you think if the people chose where our money went, that we might put more than a paltry 1% of our budget into human services? A participatory budget would allow for us to tip the scales towards equity, rather than having an administration with no vision squander our money on things that do not affect our quality of life.

Heading back to Vine Street, I want to point out something that blew my mind when I noticed it. Back in the 1800's we had a robust publicly funded and run streetcar system. The streetcar was electric, so electric lines followed each route into the suburbs. Today, there are only a few remnants of the system: the turtle-shell lights you will see behind Music Hall, on Reading Road, and throughout the city; the random tracks busting through the road on Highland Avenue; the Car Barn on Vine Street; and the old electric poles. Some of the electric poles have been converted into light poles downtown. But there's something unique about these poles from the 1800's along this little stretch of

Vine — they are holding up pieces of wood that hold the live utility lines. This is the most bootleg thing I've seen in years, which is just a reflection of how much the city values the residents of this part of Over-the-Rhine.

    I believe this is something that should cause outrage in our community. Not only has the CRC decided to close Findlay Playground without true public input, not only has the city allowed the sidewalks and lights to deteriorate, but we have probably the most unsafe and cheapest utility poles in the nation. The fact that they are from the 1800's and were made for the streetcar, not for Duke Energy, should be a real concern to everyone. How can we allow this type of disinvestment to continue? I guess we'll see what happens as 3CDC storms up Vine Street over the next few years. They have already started working on the old brewery building, and many smaller developers have already started to set their vision on creating expensive market rate housing along the corridor. Once the low-income families are pushed out, and their apartments become condos, do you think the city will keep these bootleg utility poles? Or do you think somehow, now, after 150 years, they will find the money to upgrade the poles to a safe condition?

BATTLE FOR IMAGINATION ALLEY
07/11/2019

"The first step out of oppression is expression" is a quote that Peaslee Neighborhood Center uses to emphasize the importance of the voice of the community. I have seen it attributed to long-time community changemaker, Bonnie Neumeier, who continues to educate and inspire people within, and outside, of our community today. The quote becomes more and more important each day, as the voice of the people is pushed to the side by powerful elites, such as 3CDC, the Mayor and City Manager, the Cincinnati Recreation Commission (CRC), and the Park Board. Not to mention the many developers and urbanists who are trying to craft a market-rate neighborhood at breakneck speed. It is difficult for community members to find a voice while all these powerful people are putting pressure on the neighborhood, changing it from a neighborhood of people into a profit.

On the front battle lines are the public spaces that are dwindling before our eyes. The loss of Washington, Ziegler, and Findlay Playground, the places in which community members cross paths, share stories, and express themselves, have hit us hard. Displaced from one park to another, community members are renegotiating their identities, while the fences go up around spaces used for conferencing and relaxing. The "squeeze" continues to push people out and into turf battles beyond the borders. The chaos that is created from displacement can't be measured, but the body count continues to increase as factors such as poverty, homelessness, and loneliness push people into desperate situations, such as drug use and depression.

One such public space that is currently under attack is Imagination Alley. Imagination Alley sits on the 1300 block of Vine Street, up the street from Venice on Vine, and across from buddy's place. In early 2002, according to the Over-the-Rhine Community Art Collaborative book, published in 2008, Suzanne Fischer, a local artist, saw an opportunity to reclaim the space for the community, after already working on the Peace Bench mosaic for Washington Park. The CRC site would be transformed into a bright, colorful, safe space for the community to enjoy. The arch, with artwork designed by community children, was completed and installed in 2004 and the colorful ground mosaics, "The Long and Winding Road," were designed by neighbors in drug rehabilitation programs.

The collaboration that took place involved the Art Academy, Peaslee Neighborhood Center, and hundreds of Over-the-Rhine residents. Participants were encouraged to be creative and express themselves in the mosaics, and it's worth taking a few minutes to look at the messages and images portrayed in the mosaics around the neighborhood. Unfortunately, the CRC rented out Imagination Alley for a couple of years to 3CDC so that they could park their construction equipment on it. The lease expired a couple of years ago, yet the conditions of the lease (that they would return it to the condition that it was in before the lease started) haven't been upheld, as many lights are still not functioning in the park, and the concrete and tiles remain damaged in many locations. In early 2018, 3CDC came to the Over-the-Rhine Community Council asking for approval to sell the land to 3CDC so that a business could use it for outdoor seating. The council's membership strongly opposed a full sale of the land, but was open to leasing part of the land. Ultimately, however, the process was muddied and unclear, and 3CDC essentially dropped the issue.

Imagination Alley serves as an informal backyard for many neighbors, but will be privatized and transformed by 3CDC, despite resident concerns of displacement.

Fast forward to late spring of this year, and we have a visit from a neighboring business at the Over-the-Rhine Community Council. Now, between the first 3CDC visit and this one, this business has added a permanent barrier, outdoor seating, along the sidewalk. They never came to the council with the idea of a permanent barrier blocking the sidewalk, but wanted our support for their take-over of Imagination Alley. As I am just a member of the community council, this is my perspective on what is happening, and I may be wrong, especially since I missed the last council meeting, where the business owner returned asking for a vote for the privatization of Imagination Alley.

At the first council meeting, where I was in attendance, the business owner and his father came with food to soften up the crowd. The owner made a plea that could be summed up like this: "3CDC promised us that we could have a patio on Imagination Alley, we already know who uses the space, and they are criminals (but we help people there who are in need), so it would just be better if we took over the space for our patio." And then they continued with "if we don't have a patio, our business will close, and we have expensive products, so the farmers who make our high-end food will go out of business and people will lose their jobs if we don't have a patio." There was another level of self-sacrificing going on, where the owner claimed he is paid minimum wage. They even brought drafted plans for the layout of the space. It was clear that they felt burned by the promises of 3CDC, but their lack of communication with the community council was clear by the disconnect they had in their conversation. After several questions were asked about the price points and communication with people who use the space, they ended by reiterating that they brought free food on the back table.

3CDC garbage cans line Imagination Alley's rear sidewalks.

The second council meeting didn't go well for the business either, but I was not at the meeting so what I am recounting is from several sources who attended. Once again, the pitch to privatize Imagination Alley for the restaurant's gain was made and the council had questions. The business representatives made the argument for "good guys loitering" which is a racist and anti-poor perspective that is often taken in the backdrop of gentrification. The idea is that if "good guys" use a space, it will displace the "bad guys" to other places. The concept of "loitering" was created to push Black people out of the sight of the powerful by using police resources instead of having community conversations and mutual understanding. So to add another layer to that by adding "good" is just another level of racism and classism. Community council members pushed back on the good/bad dichotomy that was being pushed.

The business also said they would do free food events in the alley if they were able to privatize it. Members asked why they didn't do this already, what is stopping them? They promised to do free-food events whether or not they received the positive vote. Observations on the spike-lined fence behind their business were made, questioning their true desire to be embraced by, and embracing of, the neighborhood. In the end, a vote was called to support the restaurant's takeover of Imagination Alley. The vote failed. The Over-the-Rhine Community Council voted to keep Imagination Alley public.

I do not believe that this issue is completely settled. 3CDC acts like they own the space today, by placing their garbage cans across the entire back line of Imagination Alley. I, personally, feel that placement of smelly 3CDC garbage on Imagination Alley is disrespectful and is intended to reduce the quality of life and use of the park. Considering the amount of time and energy that was put into Imagination Alley, to turn it into a center for profit does not abide with the community expressions that make it what it is today. It is the microaggressions, such as placing garbage cans, putting up spikes, using terms like "good guys loitering," and making promises without public input, that solidify that 3CDC is not for the community, but only seeks to increase their own wealth.

Sharp spikes line the fence around 3CDC-develcped Union Hall, bordering Imagination Alley.

THE BIG SQUEEZE
7/25/2019

Is all development good? This question comes up time and again during discussions, community meetings, and city-wide proceedings. There are some individuals who believe that $1 of investment is worth it, no matter what. With this attitude, there is no consideration for the current residents, the residents who are being displaced, workers, the built environment, or the natural environment. From my perspective, it is a dangerous viewpoint, as we are in a changing world that requires extra care and thought when doing development. So then, how can development be quantified and measured to ensure that it doesn't have an adverse effect on the community?

Fortunately, Peaslee Neighborhood Center has been studying this issue for a long time, and they recently put together the Equitable Development Rubric. (If you're not familiar with a rubric, you can think of it as a checklist with subcategories.) After doing their research, Peaslee is making recommendations on development in several areas, including: Housing Affordability, Jobs and Labor, Community Input, and Community Footprint. Just for good measure, they have an Extra Credit section that includes Diversity and Inclusion, Public Space and Infrastructure, Natural Environment, Community Organizations and Programs, and Local Enterprise. According to the Rubric, the hope is that developers and the community will "prioritize goals of equity around class and race; increase knowledge and transparency of important public processes; facilitate creative, empowering work across neighborhoods; and create a framework that equips citizens to organize for meaningful change in our local policies and practices."

We are currently feeling a real "squeeze" (as I describe it) in Over-the-Rhine. This is not a comfortable hug-type-squeeze, but more of a painful and unending squeeze. With downtown to the south, hemmed in by highways to the East and West, and the hillside with the University of Cincinnati and the hospitals to the north, Over-the-Rhine is being squeezed in on all sides. These geographic considerations, coupled with lifestyle trends and decades of public neglect, have made Over-the-Rhine a desirable, yet nearly unlivable, place to call home.

The loss of affordable housing in the neighborhood has been significant. Across the country, over the past ten years, the United States has lost most, more than 60%, of all affordable housing. The percentage lost in Over-the-Rhine continues to grow as developers claim that they must move to market-rate housing to survive. The Rubric's point system gives a clear way to score projects, including on housing affordability. If your project is exclusively market-rate, then you will receive no points. This is most likely due to the fact that we are more than 40,000 units short county-wide of affordable housing for our neighbors with the lowest incomes, yet we have more than enough housing above the area median income. To receive all four points, your project must include 65% of the units affordable at 60% AMI or less, or at least 30% of the units are affordable at 30% AMI or less. AMI means area median income. AMI can be calculated using the Neighborhood (lowest), City (middle), or County (highest) AMI, which are different from each other. The Rubric makes note of this, and shows affordable housing rents at 30% and 60% of the County AMI.

Adjacent to the former Kroger grocery site, will this development include any affordable housing?

When it comes to the labor put into the development, to score highly, you must abide by Cincinnati's Wage Theft Ordinance and all labor laws, as well as meet Ohio Prevailing Wage Contractor Responsibilities, and pay all adult employees a local living wage and meet the criteria for federal Section 3 Business Concerns, which ensure that individuals who are local, and have low incomes, are included. According to the Rubric, the highest scores can only be attained by "projects that will generate a significant number of new, post-construction jobs." While these items may seem onerous, the fact is they represent a model that does not exploit workers, particularly low-income workers, who deserve to have a living wage and protections from wage theft.

Whenever a development is proposed, it should include community input beyond an announcement of the project at a single community council meeting. To even get a single score, a developer must go beyond a community council meeting and hold an accessible public input session, take the input and rework their plans to include feedback from the public. This new plan must be re-presented at a community council. To receive the full points, the project must do everything already discussed and local, low-income residents must hold at least 20% of positions within the project's governing board. Included in the intermediary points is "support from a majority of non-profit organizations in the neighborhood that primarily serve a low-income population." These community input protocols are designed to ensure that the community has a voice in the development.

The final standalone category covers the community footprint, which includes recreation, green, and social gathering spaces, as well as, small, neighborhood-serving business, social services, housing, trees and vegetation. The goal of this section is to preserve and strengthen the use and quality of the community benefit. While this tends to lean towards the preservation of actual physical spaces, to receive the full points a development must also financially contribute "to further the positive impact of the asset(s)." The recent development on Race/15th/Pleasant is perhaps a good example of a development that did not follow this directive, as the "Field of Greens" playspace was destroyed for a gravel parking lot for construction materials.

In order for a project to be eligible for Extra Credit, they must have scored at least 50% on the previous sections. The Extra Credit will be added to the total score, opening a possible additional 20 points. In terms of Diversity and Inclusion, the City's Equal Employment Opportunity Program criteria must be met to receive a single point, and to receive the full points the 7 principles of universal design must be meaningfully incorporated, and the project must provide space available for use by the general public. For Public Space and Infrastructure there must be contributions to public funds, redevelopment of public space, be welcoming to people of all income levels, and be located in a primarily low-income area. The Natural Environment category is based upon LEED certification. To receive full points in Community Organizations and Programs, the project must be "owned and occupied by a non-profit or community based organization with the primary purpose of meeting an established community need... and low-income residents will be directly served." The last category, Local Enterprise, awards a highest score to projects that "provide commercial space to a worker-owned cooperative."

Peaslee aims at getting developers, community councils, and eventually the City, to use the Rubric when considering development in every neighborhood. The first steps have been to educate the public about the Rubric and demonstrate the need for each community. If these criteria were adopted city-wide, and used to determine where public subsidies were granted, even in cases of tax abatement, the City would be actively working towards a more equitable future. As we experience the squeeze in Over-the-Rhine, it would be more than beneficial to fully adopt and regulate development to ensure that our neighbors have a future here, in their home.

BARRIERS AND BELONGING
09/05/2019

There's nothing more special than a sense of belonging. When we grow up, we may have a small family or a large one, and we can enjoy the feeling of being part of something larger. Being a part of a family may bring us feelings of warmth, kinship, and security. Family may mean spending Sundays with your cousins growing up, or participating in family outings that create life-long memories. Once we are thrust from the nest, we are forced to create new connections through school, religion, work, and community life. When someone knows your name, remembers you, gives you an indication that they have been following your work, there is certainly a sense of pride. You want to work harder, make yourself known, and contribute to the positive events in your community. You'd do anything for your family, to make sure they feel that they are loved, while setting sensible boundaries. But what happens when you are rejected by your family?

  We know that LGBTQ youth are more likely to be rejected by their families, which leads them into homelessness. Homelessness during the teenage years means instability, and difficulty participating in typical teen things, such as sports, music, theater, school. All of those memories are shuffled together with thoughts of survival and, perhaps, even suicide. Rejection means that our youth are being approached for survival sex; they are being mistreated, and they are experiencing life-lasting trauma even before their 18th birthday. In a matter of hours, after being rejected from their families and put out on the street, the effects of PTSD begin to rewire their brains, hardening a once open and elastic mind, and create a heightened state of fight, flight, or freeze. Family rejection is perhaps one of the most cruel things that anyone can experience, simply because it is from your own kind, your own family.

  But what if the kind of rejection we experience comes from the world around us? LGBTQ folks have long experienced rejection, so we've learned to create our own communities. From the gay bars, community centers, art organizations, to house parties, tea dances, and bath houses, LGBTQ folks have been forced to find our community outside of the mainstream. The simple matter of being excluded from typical contracts (like marriage) for so long, has created a separate way in which we see the world—a world that is wrought with rejection and displacement. Rejected from our families, our social groups, our political, educational, and economic communities, we sought new ways to relate and conceptualize the world. It has also led to higher rates of drug use, risky sex, and suicide.

While many of the barriers that LGBTQ people face are structural, the fight continues for inclusion and appreciation of the views and experiences that we have. As an individual, each of us wants to bring our gifts to the world in our own way, but barriers may prevent us from fully participating in society. LGBTQ people have had to go underground because of the danger that society has posed, which is why "visibility" has become such a buzzword. Everyone needs to be seen as part of society, not shamed for just existing.

So, what does it look like when we apply a lens of rejection to race in Cincinnati. Does it look like underfunded schools that are 99% Black? Does it look like Black average income is half of white average income? Does it look like a city with no upward mobility for Black residents? Does it look like 1000 Black residents forced out of Cincinnati each year? Does it look like the denial of access to high quality health resources to Black residents? Does it look like a 20-year difference in life expectancy for Black and white residents? Does it look like disparate treatment by the police? It looks like all of these things and more, but the actual physical barriers that exclude people of color from participating in society are disturbing, to say the least.

Gates blocking off the public CRC property and sidewalk at Green and Republic Streets.

If you've been following *Streetvibes* over the past year, you have seen a couple of articles relating to Findlay Playground, sometimes known as Findlay Park. It is at Five Points on the northern border of Over-the-Rhine, at the intersection of Findlay, McMicken, and Vine Streets. The park currently has a fence around it, closing it off from use. This fence has been up for almost a year, yet the progress around the re-opening of the park has been very slow. A preliminary report draft has emerged with spurious content. The Cincinnati Recreation Commission (CRC) should be charged with neglect and dereliction of duties due to its inability to deliver on its promise to provide the space that we publicly own to the public. Due to Cincinnati Police Department (CPD) pressure, without the input of people who use the park, and without the approval of the Over-the-Rhine Community Council (OTRCC), the CRC put a fence around the park. CPD made bold, baseless claims that every person who uses the park is a criminal, and it is only used for criminal activity, yet children and families used the playground daily. A fence went up.

This is a good place to point out that the word "gentrification" simply means displacement. One group of people is displaced for another group. Closing Findlay Playground is both an act of violence by removing people from a public space, but is also a tactic of gentrification. Model Group bought the block behind the park and has already leased the public alleyway between the block and the park, and put a locked gate and fence around the alleyway. (You may remember that Model Group pushed out many people on the blocks surrounding Findlay Playground, all of them were Black people who lived there for many years, and many of them over 65 and on fixed incomes.) Model Group had a specific vision to bring affluent white people into the Findlay Market area, including their own family members. In this vision, they revamp the park to push out Black people who may live in poverty. They don't want to even see them.

So, what started with a questionable police report on the park, leading to a fence going up and slight modifications to the park, has finally led to a park-like gathering just a block south on Republic at Green Street. At that intersection, Model Group's Brickstone (perhaps now POAH controlled), Cornerstone Renter Equity, and the Over-the-Rhine Rec Center abut each other. The Rec Center has a second floor overhang, which is great for people trying to avoid a rainstorm that passes through. People who live near the corner enjoy hanging out with people who were displaced from Findlay Playground. Each day this summer, it has been a joyful place, where people listen to music, talk with each other, and enjoy the day. Personally, I walk through there regularly, and often I leave with a hug and smile, an acknowledgment. It is a park-like setting for those who were displaced.

This past month, crowd control fencing went up around the CRC and Cornerstone, blocking off the public sidewalks and parts of the publicly controlled Rec center property. This is in direct violation of human rights, and may even violate city ordinances. But, no matter what the legality or morality of the fencing, it sends a very clear message – you are not welcome, you are a nuisance, and you don't deserve a place in this community. At the last Over-the-Rhine Community Council Meeting, the police officer said the fence went up because "people gather there," not because of issues of crime, not because there was violence, simply because they exist.

"If you are Black and poor in Cincinnati, there is no place for you here." This is the message that these gates send. To think about this more deeply, contrast these gates with the bar outcroppings that take up the sidewalk on almost every street in the neighborhood. The corrals designed to keep wealthy drinkers inside the business clash with the barriers put on the sidewalk to keep people out. This is what gentrification looks like, and the violence of it; the rejection, and the racism, contribute to PTSD. Combine PTSD with the isolation that the barriers actively are trying to achieve, and you will have higher drug use, risky sexual practices, violence, and suicide. Rejection has a long-lasting effect, and until we remove the barriers that prevent people from belonging, we will be actively harming our own society.

A MICROCOSM OF HYPOCRISY
11/28/2019

Over the next year, there will be considerable discussion regarding Cincinnati's new Affordable Housing Trust Fund. By the end of 2020, we hope there will be dedicated funding sources for the trust fund, to create and sustain high-quality affordable housing in Cincinnati. The need for our trust fund came out of the steady displacement caused by gentrification in many of Cincinnati's neighborhoods. In Over-the-Rhine, Mt. Auburn, Corryville, Avondale, Lower Price Hill, Walnut Hills, and other neighborhoods, Black and low-income residents are being displaced for wealthier, and often whiter, residents and businesses. It is common knowledge that gentrification is occurring in the areas surrounding downtown, including the West End, but people often don't realize that their own taxes incentivize the displacement of residents and businesses.

Mosaic at Findlay Playground that has become inaccessible due to the privatization of Goose Alley.

The city of Cincinnati incentivizes development in many different ways, but no mechanism to prevent displacement exists. Today, a developer may receive direct subsidies from the city to develop a market-rate building. They may receive TIF funds to build a parking structure under their development. They may receive city tax breaks, amounting to millions of dollars. Developers may receive tax abatement on their property, which also short-changes our public schools. All of these tools are used to displace low-income, and often Black, residents from their homes. Other county-level pressures, such as property tax valuation, increase disparities in our communities.

In order to fully understand what is happening to our communities, we need to look at the street-level advancement of gentrification. One example of the cycle of gentrification is Findlay Playground, or as it is commonly known, Findlay Park. Parks have a huge impact on perception of a neighborhood. Looking at Washington Park, for example, which saw 46 million dollars in renovation nearly a decade ago, the privatization of the park by Cincinnati Center City Development Corporation (3CDC), received a lease of the park for 95 years. (It wasn't so simple as that, as the Cincinnati Public Schools Board agreed to a land swap to move the school land across 12th Street, where the School for Creative and Performing Arts is today. And to acquire that land, property owners, including the Drop Inn Center, had to be compensated for the historic buildings that were torn down after the residents were displaced.) 3CDC leased Washington Park from the City of Cincinnati for 95 years at the cost of $1.

Colonial brand fencing privatizes Goose Alley and prevents access to mosaic at Findlay Playground.

On the surface, the rehab of Washington Park seems like it has spurred development, increased social activities, increased revenues through parking, alcohol, and events, but there is also an insidious side that has resulted in the criminalization of people experiencing homelessness and poverty. The old park had a deep water swimming pool, including a swim and dive team made up of Over-the-Rhine youth. The basketball court and non-magnet elementary school (which was the highest performing in the neighborhood) were all removed as well. As the closed-door community meetings on the rehab of the park began to show the loss of these important community assets, the protest included signs and chants of "You can't learn to swim in a sprayground!" which show that the lack of access to swimming pools in neighborhoods like this result in drowning later in life. This is especially true for Black people, who have been historically barred from swimming pools. (Coney Island even closed their pool for several years, rather than let Black children swim in it.)

Corner store closes without fanfare, due to unexpected Findlay Playground closure.

Also concerning are the rules that 3CDC put on the park which bar people and organizations from donating clothes, food, and having events that benefit people in poverty. Essentially, criminalizing homelessness by banning laying down in the park or eating out of garbage cans creates a very real barrier for people who want to use the park, as it was intended, a respite from the bustle of city life. Coupled on top of complaints from people experiencing homelessness and housing insecurity who have been "banned" from using the bathrooms in the park, it is clear that the hostile designed fence around the park isn't the only thing keeping the "undesirables" out of the park — the 24/7 private security force is always at work.

The renovations of Ziegler Park proved to directly displace Black residents from the area, both in privately-owned apartments, and subsidized apartments abutting the park. We have seen the cost of a swim membership rise from $4 a year to $4 a day. While there are claims that children can get discounted rates, this comes with structural and racist barriers that require family background information which result in less accessibility for all families. Overall, the millions that went into these two parks means that someone has made a considerable profit off of the projects.

At a recent community meeting about Findlay Playground, that was attended by less than a dozen residents, we heard that the goal is to raise 22 million dollars for the rehab. The CRC Director of Recreation stated that the Cincinnati Business Committee will ask the State of Ohio for 5 million, and the rest would be from TIF money and other fundraising channels. The Director said that they don't need any plans to present to the State for the 5 million dollars, and at this time have no idea what the 22 million dollars rehab would actually look like. The purpose of the meeting was to come up with programming ideas, starting in April of 2020, so that if the fence is removed, there would be programs set in place. It was clear that it doesn't take millions to remove the fence.

The Director of Recreation also said that the reason the fence was put up was due to safety concerns of the Mayor, City Manager, and the Cincinnati Police Department. While Grant Park, just a few blocks away, also sees high crime, including murder, there is no fence around it. The area around Fountain Square sees more crime than these areas, but there is no fence around it. People in our community bemoan the loss of any parking spots, but when the "City Parking Only" signs in front of Findlay Playground went up, no one mentioned it as an issue. When the public mosaic was gated off by Model Group on the west side of the park, no one said anything regarding the loss of public art, yet we are filling every space with murals for BLINK and ArtWorks. Finally, when the word on the street is that the store directly across Vine from the park closed because the owner said they lost all of their business when the fence went up around the park, no one came to their aid, even though the community acts like small, minority-owned businesses are a priority. (A recent report shows that only about 8% of the businesses in Over-the-Rhine currently are Black owned, even though the neighborhood is still majority Black).

While the condos abutting the Park receive tax abatement for decades and other incentives to displace the low-income Black residents who lived there less than 2 years ago, the neighbors get a fence around their park. When white people make blatantly racist remarks, even micro-aggressions, at every community meeting, the true meaning of the fence is explicated: Only power and money is welcome, everyone else is fenced off.

IT'S A WRAP
11/14/2019

The struggle to preserve, maintain, and build affordable housing in our county continues, as we are more than 40,000 units short of affordable housing in Hamilton County. As we gear up for a ballot initiative to get the City's support of the Affordable Housing Trust Fund, it's important to examine some of the issues that have brought us to this crisis. When it comes to homelessness, we know that

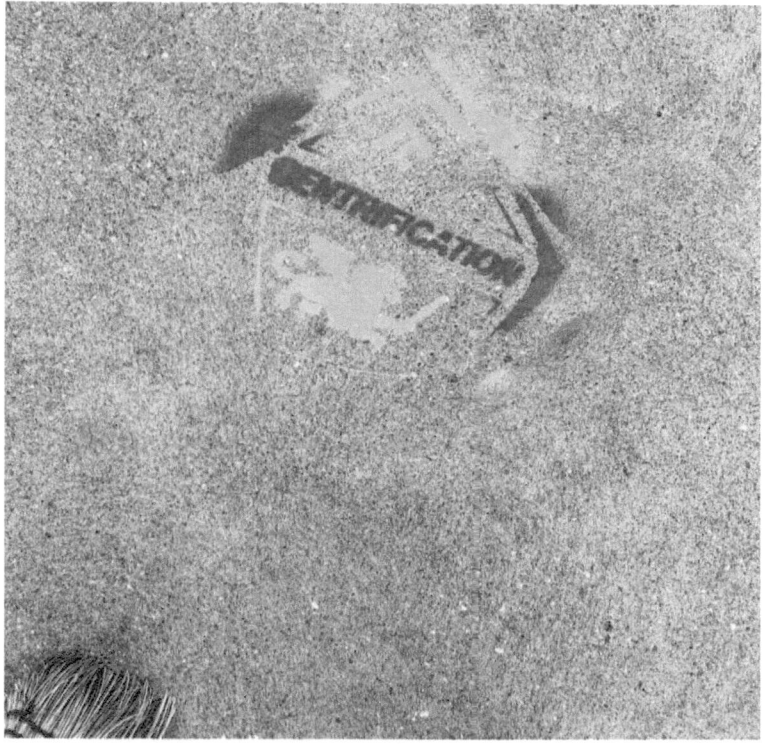

Like a broom, gentrification sweeps through the neighborhood, removing what, and who, those in power deem undesirable.

the lack of affordable housing, the lack of a livable wage, and the lack of housing protections have combined together to create our housing crisis. Coupled with disinvestment in public housing for over three decades, the options for housing have shifted greatly in favor of the wealthy and rich. But there is, however, an advantage that proponents of affordable housing have in our favor — the power of the people.

Recently, the FC Cincinnati and Port Authority commissioned a "study" of housing in the West End neighborhood of Cincinnati. This work was not done out of consideration of the community, but rather was required following the hasty, and possibly unjust, Community Benefits Agreement (CBA) that was produced and agreed upon by the wealthy and affluent stakeholders following community outrage. The West End, and neighboring communities, like Over-the-Rhine, expressed deep and valid concerns about putting a private stadium on top of an existing public school stadium and street. Many of the concerns rightfully stemmed from the tens of millions of public funds that are aiding the development of this private stadium. Other justified concerns came out of the historical knowledge that the majority of residents from the West End have been displaced from the neighborhood at least twice. Seeing the importance of retaining the fabric of the community, residents fought back against the stadium, but were ultimately thwarted by the ruling class, including City Councilmember, PG Sittenfeld, who pushed the project through against the wishes of the majority — both community councils, the West End and Over-the-Rhine voted against the stadium's presence.

Throughout the past couple of years, since the powerful Lindner and Farmer families business, FC Cincinnati, has been forced upon a neighborhood that did not want it to come, the amount of racism, whether aware or not, that the company has levied against the neighborhoods has been astonishing. Everything from questioning the validity of the community council votes, silencing the voices of those who are concerned, encouraging their supporters to say racist things at the school board meeting, like "Imagine it's 2034, and 'Keisha' from the West End is on the American Olympic soccer team because she had the chance to play soccer." Ultimately, the responsibility of the destruction of the community will lay in the hands of a corporation, known as FC Cincinnati.

A Community Benefits Agreement is intended to be a document that gives the community the power to retain the values of the community while giving a developer, or developers, a guide as to how to appropriately interact with the neighborhood. As part of the CBA, which was rushed through during a private weekend meeting, a housing study was required. The FC Cincinnati business was advised to pay $100,000 to fund the housing study. In comparison, the company paid $150,000,000 to join the Major League Soccer league. Apparently, one hundred thousand dollars wasn't enough to fully fund the study, so The Port put money towards the study as well. Both of these entities own property in the West End and plan to make as much money as possible off of their investments. The Port can even acquire properties through eminent domain, as long as it is done for an authorized purpose. The footing on which this housing study stands is shaky, at best, as those who paid for the study intend to gain financially from its recommendations.

In the boundaries section of the housing study, Over-the-Rhine is referred to as an "affluent neighborhood" although the majority of residents in the neighborhood live in poverty. This statement shows how little regard the study authors have towards people living in poverty in our communities.

Central Avenue, a public asset as a street, is the future site of the FC Stadium (Soccer), with Wade Street in background.

It shows how little a voice and power the authors believe that people living in poverty have to make decisions regarding their own futures. Ultimately, this disdain for low-income, generally Black residents pours into all parts of the study. While the study shows that the area median income for the neighborhood is $14,632, the proposed solutions do not directly enable this group of people to retain membership in the neighborhood.

In the Displacement Risk Analysis section, the study inaccurately states that people living in subsidized housing are not at risk of being pushed out of the neighborhood. Public housing across the country is being privatized through a program called RAD. Without going into a great deal of detail on RAD, it's important to note that there is an "acceptable loss" of units through the RAD process, and possible loopholes that will allow for entire buildings to be razed without the requirement to rebuild them. Stanley Rowe Tower, for example, has had considerable pressure on it to be razed in recent history. The other problem with the assumption that people in subsidized housing are safe from displacement doesn't take into account that Cincinnati Metropolitan Housing Authority (CMHA) evicts more people than anyone else in our county. It is clear that these numbers greatly conceal the actual vulnerability of residents of the West End. One ominous statement appears in the study "If nothing is done and if no policy or recommendations are implemented, then the risk of displacement could exponentially increase with the expiration of subsidized rental units."

The study acknowledges that the vast majority of residents wish to remain in the West End. We have seen through the Wade and Central Streets tenant organization, Fight Back Cincinnati, that people want to remain connected to their neighborhood and social ties. Leaving the neighborhood represents a social death, and is made even more difficult with the lack of available affordable housing. The housing crisis makes displacement even more dangerous, as people are forced to settle for substandard housing far away from their known social circles. Gentrification is a type of genocide which gives the power and control into the hands of the wealthy while pushing residents on fixed and low incomes from the neighborhood.

Two housing production scenarios are presented: 1. Meet the current need for housing; 2. Meet the potential displacement need for housing. The numbers that are presented, in regard to percentage of Area Median Income (AMI) are based upon county AMI, rather than neighborhood AMI. County AMI is $78,300, whereas you remember that the neighborhood AMI is $14,632. Therefore, the proposals for housing are not for existing residents, but rather investors who are bringing with them wealth from outside of the neighborhood. The first housing production scenario calls for 456 rental units above 80% AMI, meaning that you would have to make at least $62,000 per year to afford; 55 units at or below 50% AMI, meaning you would have to make $39,000 per year to afford; and 148 ownership units above 100% AMI, meaning you would have to make at least $78,000 per year to afford. This scenario clearly does not stop the loss of our neighbors, but only encourages development of high-end units at the expense of existing residents. The second scenario, which claims that it will prevent the loss of existing residents, requires 869 rental units at or below 50% AMI to be built; however, this does not take into account the residents who are most vulnerable, those who are living in subsidized housing threatened by RAD and evictions, but it does show the great need for affordable housing in the neighborhood.

Unfortunately, in the end, once the majority of low income Black residents are displaced from the West End and the luxury apartments and condos are built and filled with white suburban-bred "urban pioneers," the gentrification of the West End will be seen as a success, just as "the affluent" Over-the-Rhine is described today. In Over-the-Rhine, we have lost thousands of low income units, and more than half of the Black population over the past 17 years, and somehow this is being lauded as a success. We continue to fight back against displacement and the unbridled power of white generational wealth as we see fit; however, only through true system change, such as the affordable housing trust fund, will be actually able to change the direction of housing from loss to gain.

CHAPTER 4: SYSTEMATIC LOSS OF COMMUNITY COHESION

POLITICS OF PROTEST
7/15/2016

I see you. When you are silent, when you hide, I am aware of your presence. Injustice anywhere is an injustice everywhere... right? Last month, when a gunman killed 49 people in Orlando, mostly white, gay people called for a larger police presence at Pride Celebrations. I was not one of them.

    I have been clashing with the police since I can remember – as a teen, I was speaking out against the racist enforcement of teen-curfews and their placement in our public schools. As I entered college, I found myself struggling against them again in our small college town, as they racially profiled my Black classmates, harassing them, and making them feel unwelcome. I stood up to them when they insisted on doing "rounds" through the residence halls. I told them that guns are not welcome in our home. After some phone calls, they complied. Our halls became safe again.

    I worry about this upcoming election because our American Memory is so short. People don't remember the tens of thousands that took to the street when George Bush took (stole) office in 2001. We don't remember because it was not reported on in the media. Few remember the horrible conditions we faced protesting the RNC in New York City in 2004. Hundreds locked in storage containers on the docks, kept over the 48 hours required by law to see a judge, charged with nothing.

    When Bush came to Union Terminal in 2003 to announce his plan to attack Iraq, I was impressed by the thousands that showed up along Ezzard Charles to protest war. I was surprised that people of all walks of life stood up to say "war is not the answer." We were tired, September 11, 2001 happened when we were still picking up the pieces of Officer Roach's murder of Timothy Thomas. Roach, who was so scared for his life that he chased and killed Thomas, rather than stopping and finding safety. Cincinnati police were called to task by the Department of Justice – nearly 100 violations of practices and procedures *on the books*, and people still thought it was more important to look at Thomas' non-violent record, than the Roach family's history of racism or a system that thrives on suffering.

When Bush came to the Union Terminal fundraiser, ready to announce war, we took the streets, and blocked the entrance. I began to think about Rev. Maurice McCrackin's refusal to use his legs when he was arrested at the White House. I vowed to never let the police take me – and if they did, they would need to carry me away. When the police horses came to push us back, I sat down in the street, within moments, hundreds of others sat down – and we refused to move. We sat there the entire length of the event, and as wealthy benefactors tried to leave, we blocked them. The police used the horses as weapons, almost pushing people into I-75. Sadly, today some people, including Council Members, are calling for a return of the mounted patrols.

I spent most of the Bush years in protest – Cincinnati, Chicago, Columbus, New York, Washington D.C. – these became my second homes. I fear that we'll be in the same situation if Trump is elected. At the 2005 Inauguration, Bush became so scared that he put up a 10 foot fence along the parade route. Legend goes that there were more police than square feet in DC that day. I knew what to expect since I had seen police throw old women to the ground in 2001, people being sprayed with chemical irritant, and unmarked school buses used as funnels to reduce the crowds. I didn't expect the 10 foot fence and the police spraying us with canons filled with chemical irritant. I had already been schooled by my socialist friends to treat the police as workers, and not see them for the system they uphold and represent. So, as they sprayed a group of people peacefully praying (through the fence), I yelled at them "Be Professional!" and repeated the chant over and over. It seemed as though the officers were enjoying it as they sprayed everyone who walked by, even people randomly leaving their hotels. As we regrouped to flush out our eyes with milk and show solidarity for those who were arrested, I felt hopeless since I knew we had four more years of Bush policy, obstructionism, and systematic violence.

On the surface, we may seem like we've come a long way since 2005. But, we lost so many rights during the War on Terror that we've come to accept them. If police were really created to maintain wealth and specifically to catch people who were considered property, it is no surprise to me that police departments are paying people to improve their image. The "Running Man Challenge," while completely ironic and inappropriate for a police department to do, is just a way to distract you from the massive amount of inequalities that the police uphold.

A couple of years ago, I was involved in a DWB (driving while Black) incident that was something out of a bad made-for-tv movie. Pulled over on

Liberty Street, surrounded on all sides by police, hunkering down behind their cruiser doors, packing their shotguns in front of us, and pointing them ever-so-intently on our vehicle. In the end, the BMV (Ohio Bureau of Motor Vehicles) had some inaccurate data, but the psychological damage was done. Being thrown in the back of a police cruiser, having your identity questioned, and then once confirmed "let go" with no apology. The result of the citizen complaint was threefold: 1. "if you point your camera phone at an officer, we will assume it's a weapon;" 2. "if we (the police) didn't follow what the system told us to do, we'd be reprimanded," and most importantly, 3. "being a Black male is the only description necessary." Age, height, weight, hair – none of that matters to police.

Yes, the system is broken – from the BMV, police procedures, war machine, racism, classism, generational poverty, homophobia, etc. But a large part of the problem is the code of silence that police officers follow. There is no other industry where people don't call out each other for messing up… and very few industries take people's lives without impunity. The first step to solving a problem is to admit that it exists. Until our police admit there is a problem, there will be no solution. More than a third of our city's budget goes to the police. Over 60% of our budget goes to public safety. How can we expect the powerless to change the powerful? Nearly 600 people will have been killed by U.S. police this year by the time you read this. I would be surprised if more than five are taken to trial this year. Most officers will have a GoFundMe site up within 24 hours, a guaranteed retirement, or a promotion to a quiet suburb. Take time to educate yourself and get involved with the Homeless Coalition and the Black Lives Matter movement.

THE SINGULARITY: WHAT MATTERS TO HISTORY
07/29/2016

The printing press. The Magna Carta. Abolishing the institution of slavery. Radio transmissions. The Great Depression. The moon landing. Color television. Brown vs. the Board of Education. The internet. 9/11. Pokémon GO or Alton Sterling?

Thousands march for Black Lives Matter in Cincinnati.

When we look at our collective history, there are times when you can't "put the paste back into the tube" and we simply can't go back to the way things were before. These moments in time are called "singularities" and often result in a shift, or change in the way people view the world. Sometimes we talk about a paradigm shifting, or a new technology, in a way that is so casual, but in reality, these are the things that the future generations will never know life without.

When I was growing up, we still listened to the radio and taped our favorite songs. These were the original mix tapes, and they were full of blips and bleeps from people walking around the room or losing the signal due to a storm. Today, we just turn on YouTube and listen to what we want. We can even use AdBlock to get rid of commercials, or pay a few bucks to watch television without commercials. This is a radical shift from waiting to watch something after school, on a small television, with a third of the time full of commercials. We can't go back to cassette tapes and VHS now that everything is digital. Analog died slowly but is completely unknown to Millennials, marking the shift towards digital.

A few weeks ago, in *Streetvibes*, I made an obvious prediction that there would be another person of color killed by a white police officer, but what I didn't predict was the outrage. I have been following the work of the *Guardian*'s Counted project, that counts and catalogues all the civilians who are killed by the police in the United States. To put this in perspective, a newspaper from the United Kingdom is documenting the terror of our police departments because there is no governmental body, organization, project, or program that requires police departments to report on the number of people they kill. We should be outraged that we are not the ones keeping track of our own house.

When video surfaced of Alton Sterling being executed in a gas station parking lot it seemed as though we were starting to see a real paradigm shift: white people peeked through the veil of abuse that power hungry police officers have been inflicting on Black, brown, and female bodies for hundreds of years (or what feels like hundreds of years). The Black Lives Matter movement saw a uptick of white people who started to say enough is enough, but was this month a true singularity, or will police business continue as normal?

Also this July, Pokémon GO was released. It is a mobile video game (played on phones) where players actually go to parks, cemeteries, and walk down the street to "catch" virtual monsters. The goal is to collect 250 pocket monsters (Pokémon) in the streets, parks, and cemeteries throughout our community. While there has been some serious problems with the premise (going out into public while using your phone), there have also been some life-changing things: kids with social disorders out in the street making new friends, leaving the house; people making connections; seeing new places in your own community; parks packed all day. Jokingly, people have said that First Lady, Michelle Obama, was behind it since she has been fighting teenage obesity. Is it possible that the face of video games will change from the pasty white faces of mom's basement to the sun-kissed, social faces of neighbors in a community? Or will the glamour wear off and the monster seekers find themselves back in their basements and game rooms, playing games that kill, rob, and abuse virtual others?

When we are privileged enough to witness a singularity in our lifetimes, it is important to question who benefits from it. The effect of a single event will never fully be realized, but it is up to us to guide future generations and protect them from systematic oppression. Will July 2016 be known for a shift in the public's acceptance of state-sponsored killing or a video game that puts people out of their houses and into the community?

BEING BRAVE IN FREEDOM LAND
09/09/2016

In my last article, I used some of Melissa Mosby's words to describe the situation that she saw while living on the streets. One thing that she describes is a "puffy pink cloud" that people want to live in that allows them to ignore reality. As we get closer to the election, I see more and more people encouraging people on the left to *stop* protesting and do something for their community.

It's frustrating to me, as someone who has seen the results of protest, that people would attempt to silence anyone – let alone people who are trying to get on even footing. It's even more frustrating that when people who are speaking the truth are called "protestors" and "activists" when those who funnel money from our public wealth are called industrious or successful businesses. Someone who feels they are above the law and shouldn't pay taxes, is not only short-sighted, but also ignorant of the benefits and opportunities our society has created for them.

Other than the election, other events have sparked this conversation. People accused American football player Colin Kaepernick of being against the military when he didn't stand up for the National Anthem. This act of protest, which is exactly the type of protest that was written about 150 years ago by Henry David Thoreau, encourages people to think critically about what it means to be an American and what it means to live in a "free country." At the time, Thoreau was upset by the institution of slavery and by the Mexican-American War. Through his writing, Thoreau has inspired countless others to do something – even to just speak their mind – when they witness or encounter injustice. Kaepernick's act of civil disobedience sparked a wide discussion about what it means to be a patriot – but also what the writer of the anthem – a white person who lawfully owned people – meant when he wrote the National Anthem. While up to interpretation, there is a piece of the poem that isn't sang in the anthem that references "slave(s)" and their inability to gain freedom.

In 2003, my brother was sent to Iraq in the first wave of Marines who went to secure the oil fields for U.S. production interests. Since we were kids, my brother has been my best friend and someone who I look up to. When he joined the military in 2000, Clinton was president and no one thought we would go to war again for our own interests, so he didn't think joining the reserves would put him in harm's way. When he was sent, he fulfilled his duty, by helping to set up a police academy in Iraq on the border with Syria, during several deployments. When you have a family member in the service, so many things remind you of how much you miss them. For me, when I pulled into a gas station, I would become upset that this is why he was gone, for an unjust war to bring oil home from the Gulf. I couldn't take it, so I got rid of my car and began to walk, ride my bike, and enjoy life more. It gave me a way to ground myself in my community – I couldn't just jump in my car and go to another city when things were too much in Cincinnati. I was here, and this community was what I was going to make of it.

Also during that time, I sat during every national anthem. Graduations – sat. Sporting events – sat. Political events – sat. It was difficult at first as I was glared at, but every time it got easier, and I was able to create in my head, reasons why it was my right to do this. I had felt my country let me down. And beyond the war, it has continued to let me down. We could be a country of greatness, but we are too concerned with protecting the rich and pathologizing poverty. Pushing people to the margins, and denying rights and services to people who don't fit a certain mold.

What this all boils down to in my mind is the differences in how we understand the word "freedom." Erich Fromm, who witnessed first-hand the Nazi movement in Germany, notes that there is a difference between "freedom from" and "freedom to" and this difference, in my opinion, offers us an opportunity to critically think about what America represents to us and to the entire world. Do you think the world sees criticism of Kaepernick as more or less American than his protest? Do we provide a community that gives people the freedom to work, live, love in ways that are most beneficial to themselves, or do we only give people freedom from certain forms of overt oppression? We actively oppress people in this country through voter disenfranchisement, marriage laws, the preschool to prison pipeline, etc.; however, ultimately, we can never be truly free of our responsibilities to our families, communities, and our country. So how can we be free to reimagine what freedom looks like when the rules are so rigid?

Much of the criticism thrown at Kaepernick has related his skin color, his family dynamic, and his wealth. People have said that he is ungrateful and doesn't understand what he is doing. Another football player criticized him for not being "Black." This brought up a good point about advocacy, and how it relates to those of us in the Black Lives Matter movement who are white. This reminds me of Anne Braden, who fought hard to desegregate Louisville, who talked about why she got into the movement. It wasn't because of how the system treated Black people, she said, but how it treated the poor whites. She knew in her heart that if the system treated them *this* badly, it would be much worse for her Black neighbors. She understood advocacy and exercised her freedom to create a better world for her entire community. This came at a great cost to her, after having a cross burned in her front yard and later tried for sedition, she was blacklisted from employment and ostracized from her community. Her freedom "from" was not granted for many decades, and systemically the effect of redlining certainly continues to this day.

James Baldwin, the great American writer of the 20th Century, acknowledged the realization that Black people have when they are forced to pledge allegiance to a flag of a country that hasn't shown allegiance to Black people. And it is in times like this when we are reminded that "the Land of the Free" is drastically different from "the Home of the Brave."

THE WORST IS YET TO COME
04/14/2017

Walking around Over-the-Rhine this week, I felt as though we, as a country, are such hypocrites, liars, and crooks. On Vine Street, people casually streamed out of the donut and ice cream shops, celebrating spring break. People from the suburbs sauntered down the street with bags of donuts and ice cream cones in hands, trying to lick them before they melt, or at least save the donuts until they get home. Meanwhile, we dropped a historically large bomb on Afghanistan. We launched dozens of missiles into Syria, and continued dropping bombs across the globe.

I know there is mass suffering here at home – people being displaced from their long-time homes so that developers can move the rich, or even their families, into the neighborhood. Instead of starting with the 500 abandoned buildings in Over-the-Rhine, they set their sights on the easily flippable buildings and pushed thousands out of the neighborhood. Coupled with the direct gentrification, we are seeing mass indirect gentrification – with the schools, the Laundromats, the post office, the hardware store, friends, and family all pushed out of the neighborhood… all of this contributes to homelessness. And so does war.

We are sitting back in our easy chairs having debates of whether we should take asylum-seekers and refugees because they may be dangerous – when we are the largest producers of war in the world. We produce the most ammunition, machines of war, the ships, and of course, the missiles. We'll sell to both sides of a conflict. Our wealth in this country is so connected with war that we put the majority of our budgets into war – including locally. We spend more on the police than anything else – yet homicides increase and the streets remain dangerous. Why is this? Are we in complete denial? Possibly.

We need to start changing our perspective and learn how to stand behind our stated values – freedom, happiness, prosperity. Currently, we are quick to blame victims of the system and act like they have some chance. When I hear talk about homelessness (which is necessary), I see how off-base people tend to be regarding solutions. When students decide that a barrier to being housed is transportation, because you know, "they can't get to their job" it makes me realize that there is a serious barrier to understanding systematic causes and the symptoms of homelessness.

We don't have a livable wage, so you can work day and night and still not be able to afford a two bedroom apartment. You can save up all your money, and still not be able to pay your bills and feed your family. Yet, we'll be quick to villainize someone who uses alcohol to numb their pain, yet think it's totally ok for someone to go home after work and crack open a beer every night – in fact you are rewarded when you go to Happy Hours and other work-related activities. It's a double standard.

Without a conscience, we drop bombs on Brown and Black communities across the globe. Afghanistan is still one of the most impoverished countries in the world. The bombs we drop are probably valued more than the entire country's GNP. I don't know the numbers (and many aren't recorded because of drug trade), but I can almost guarantee it. What do you think is the connection between the poppy fields in Afghanistan and the heroin crisis? How do those drugs get here?

I didn't think it would be right to let this time of war go by without writing something about it. I can't speak for everyone, but I hope that we know that with every bomb we drop, we create more enemies. One day, perhaps in the near future, we will be asked to be responsible for what we've done. Until then, we'll exploit war for ratings. When we believe more is better, rather than fair is better, we enforce racist power structures, and give them value. We must change our entire perspective to bring about peace.

IS A PICTURE WORTH A THOUSAND HOMES?
07/07/2017

What do you think about the ArtWorks murals throughout the city? Have you ever participated in an event that involved one or more murals? Have you ever connected with one in a meaningful way, or do you just see them as frivolous art? Sometimes, as with most art, there is more than meets the eye. This summer's new projects are no different.

Does art improve the quality of life? Magnetic board with a statement about life.

Awhile back, a pro-education, anti-gun mural went up at Christ Church Cathedral's downtown location. Prominently displayed on 4th Street was a mural with men holding giant pencils. The pencils were placed where guns once were in the photo, as you can see in the image from episcopaldigitalnetwork.com. To some, the image was controversial, and the artists ICY and SOT were asked to do another mural this summer here in Cincinnati.

Iranian-born, New York City-based artists, ICY and SOT are two brothers who have endured the wrath of their home government, and are now considered refugees in America. They have family in Baltic states and scattered around the world, but they knew that coming to America would change the way they are able to do their artwork. I had the pleasure of taking them on a social justice walking tour of Over-the-Rhine to help inform their new work.

During our walk, I asked them a lot of questions about their work, their transition to American life, and their life before coming here. They were forced into political prisons and treated without humanity, which ultimately informs the work that they do. They marveled at our architecture, and how much things had changed since they were here just 3 years ago. They said Over-the-Rhine looked unfamiliar to them.

Mural celebrating iconic locations and buildings in neighborhood with added hands.

Their first design attempt at the new mural fell flat. The Homeless Coalition was asked to bring a speaker to the incoming ArtWorks Apprentices (high school and early college students who work through the summer to paint the new murals). ArtWorks was happy to let me know that they are doing a new mural to combat the stereotypes of people experiencing homelessness. The other goals of the mural were very lofty, but great goals: raise awareness about homelessness and get people to engage in the fight for affordable housing. We stood by these goals, but not the design.

The initial design was simply a shirtless African-American man with windows painted into his body. One of my colleagues remarked that it was more a semblance to slavery than housing issues. Others thought that if we want people to see and act on homelessness, then putting windows on a person's body instructs people to "look through" rather than "see" them. Through a series of random events, ArtWorks heard about our concerns and invited us to meet with the artists when they came in town – which led to my tour.

During our hour walk, we showed them the mural projects that missed the mark. One of them is on Vine Street, which shows landmarks in the neighborhood. When residents asked to have humans in the mural, ArtWorks placed some disembodied arms in the mural to try to assuage the community. We talked to the artists about how this is not a solution, but a missed opportunity to hear and react accordingly to community voices.

Today, the mural work continues on the side of the Recovery Hotel, on the 1200 block of Vine Street. The mural will be opposite the Cincinnati Strong Man mural, and will contain several, clothed persons with ambiguous racial backgrounds. We know that African Americans are over-represented in homelessness because of the continued legacy of American racism, including redlining and other, more contemporary, barriers. It will also include a couple small surprises that tie it to the neighborhood, as well as, signs to raise awareness about homelessness.

Faces of Homelessness mural work on the side of the Recovery Hotel.

Strategies to End Homelessness is the sponsor of the mural, which is on an Over-the-Rhine Community Housing building. Along with ArtWorks, these two organizations had final approval of the design. Strategies wrote that the new mural will include people who have experienced homelessness here in Cincinnati. As we are 40,000 units short on Affordable Housing, I can only hope this helps us in our goal to create a local Affordable Housing Trust Fund.

CINCINNATI'S CRISIS MODE
09/09/2017

Have you ever woken up refreshed after a night's rest? Are you able to leave work and picture the door "closed" and not think about it at all while you are home? Are you able to pay your rent on the first of every month without worrying about bouncing your check? Do you have the food you want in your kitchen, when you want it? What if you were constantly worried about these things with no hope for change? You'd be in a state of crisis.

The world in which we live thrives on crisis. Educational theorists believe that there are a series of "crisis" events that we must pass through to get to new stages in our development. A crisis literally changes our brains to where we have options to reject, accept, or assimilate our new found perspective. It is at times very daunting, but we generally get through the crisis and have a chance to decompress, celebrate our failures (or successes), and move on to something else. But, for people experiencing homelessness and poverty, crisis mode is the norm, not the exception.

Having to figure out what and where you are going to eat (if at all), or where you are going to sleep, or if you can even sleep because you are so stressed out, is more than stressful – as Streetvibes Distributor Willa Jones, poet and writer, explains in her poem "Intoxication," you can be intoxicated without taking a drink because your mind is so preoccupied with survival that it's impossible to think clearly. How can you think about tomorrow when your basic needs aren't met today?

And this type of crisis-thinking isn't limited to people experiencing homelessness. Housing, which seems like it should be a basic right, is both fragile and continuously contested. According to a recent LISC study, 55,000 families are trying to get into 15,000 units of affordable housing in Hamilton County. We are, whether or not you recognize it in your daily life, in a community-wide crisis. We are in a severe housing crisis that benefits only a very few wealthy landowners and developers, while leaving the rest of us fighting with our neighbors.

And we have a wider crisis in Cincinnati – racism – which negatively affects us all. In the study The State of Black Cincinnati, released a couple of years ago, it showed that the reality for people of color in Cincinnati is so far removed from that of white Cincinnati, that there's no surprise white people have no clue on the experience of people of color in this city. Black people have severely lower health and education outcomes, but more shockingly (because America is touted as a meritocracy) upward mobility for Black people in Cincinnati simply doesn't exist. There is no path out of poverty for thousands upon thousands of Cincinnati's residents. No path at all.

Until we start to recognize the fact that white people have all the chances and privileges in this city, and we begin to understand how much that holds ALL OF US back, we will continue to demonize and scapegoat the downtrodden, while falsely celebrating our successes (which were violently pulled from the potential success of Black people.) We must start to recognize structural violence, which, to me, is a continuation of redlining, Jim Crow, and ultimately slavery. As a city, we, including what seems to be the business community in Cincinnati, haven't moved on from white supremacy. It would be a huge step to get everyone to recognize that we have created, and actively maintain, a crisis of immense proportions.

If I had all the answers I wouldn't be open to learning and seeing more. I do know that we must create a more stable and fair community. Affordable Housing Advocates, a local group of housing providers, advocates and consumers dedicated to the goal of ensuring good, safe, accessible, affordable housing for all people in Southwest Ohio, is working vigilantly on an housing trust fund which will help create and preserve affordable housing in Cincinnati. We hope to get the county to start a program as well.

POLICE STATE TERROR
05/04/2018

For most of my life, the only nightmares I had were dreams where the police showed up. I would struggle to wake myself up whenever they arrived on the scene. Waking up in a pool of sweat, I would find myself thanking my body for allowing myself to wake up from the nightmare. As a white person in America, it was just a dream — but for Black people, it's a daily reality.

All of us feel a rush, a mix of fear, excitement, and shame, when the red, blue, and white lights appear on the interstate behind us. "Am I speeding? Did I change lanes illegally? Please don't pull up behind me." When the cruiser passes us by, we release a sigh of relief, wipe the sweat off our brows with clammy hands. Now imagine if those feelings were constant no matter where you are and what you are doing — this is the experience for Black people in America today.

It all makes sense when you consider the history of policing. Sheriff patrols evolved from chattel slavery when people were legally considered property, and bounties were placed, not just on the heads of specific people, but upon an entire race of people — Black people. Even the 13th Amendment, which outlawed most slavery, allows for people who are imprisoned to be used as slaves who create products that you and I purchase every day. Ultimately, this system of inequality is built on a foundation of capitalism, and the police are the executors of property protection.

If the function of the police is to protect property, then what form does it take? Recently, I have noticed an increase of patrols, arrests, and harassment in the northern part of Over-the-Rhine. Cruisers tucked into alleyways or doing rounds around the block, bicycle police stopping on abandoned lots, arresting people. Less than a mile away, in the West End, police are passing out flyers saying that the area is dangerous and people may face federal charges if they are caught in the area. This partnership with the ATF has been going on for years, and the Cincinnati Police have claimed that this is not part of the FC Cincinnati stadium being forced on the neighborhood. I disagree — it's all connected as the process of gentrification takes many forms, and certainly the presence of the police is part of the removal of low-income Black people from the neighborhood. Police harassment is part of the strategy.

The fact remains that the police do not help people rise out of poverty, but in fact create poverty. When students are harassed by the police in Clifton, the contact with the police creates a paper trail that will haunt them for the rest of their lives. When Black people are pulled over, even as passengers in a car, they are treated as criminals, and this may be recorded as an arrest, even though they aren't charged with anything. For people of color, simple contact with the police may show up on background checks, preventing access to work or housing. This is a separate world for white people, who don't have to worry about any of this at all because things get recorded differently and white people have the opportunity to defend themselves against accusations.

Recently, I was involved in a "routine traffic stop" after the CPD were scanning license plates on Main Street. I will just summarize one thing that I learned from it. I felt that the police treated the driver, who is Black, unfairly, so I filed a complaint with the Citizen's Complaint Authority whose official response was that the only description the police needed was "Black and Male." Age, weight, height were not factors that needed to be considered. This system is built to suppress people of color at every turn, and the police are the major actors who have systematized harassing and, ultimately, killing, whether quickly or slowly, people of color.

Finding ways to cope with police terror are imperative for people of color. Whether it be through learning self-defense, learning law, or tactics in dealing with the police (such as putting your wallet, registration, etc., on the dashboard so you don't have to reach for anything), Black people in Cincinnati are forced to create ways to physically and mentally protect themselves — a terror white people can never understand.

CHAPTER 5: HOMELESSNESS AND GENTRIFICATION

COUNTING ON US...
1/15/2016

Twice a year, the Homeless Coalition participates in the PIT Count with our member organizations, such as PATH and the VA. The PIT Count stands for Point-in-Time, which essentially means finding and counting people who are living outside, in encampments, or in shelters. I took part in my first PIT Count in September, when we attempted to get an accurate count of the number of individuals living outside at the end of the summer. Organizations are required by HUD to do a PIT Count during a cold night in January, but the actual effect of it is greater than just a count.

While I'm not looking forward to being out in the cold this month, I have to be realistic and compassionate to those who spend every night outside. However, I am looking forward to developing relationships with people and working as part of a team to complete the count this month. The following are some of my reflections on the first PIT Count I participated in last year.

I was fortunate to not have much warning about the PIT Count – I think it was during my first week with the Homeless Coalition. It didn't give me an opportunity to stress about it. We met at the Coalition to form teams to split up between the downtown business district and Over-the-Rhine. Before we left, we were told about the importance of keeping the locations confidential because there are people out there who might target individuals who are experiencing homelessness. It's important to realize just how vulnerable people are when they are sleeping outside – not only to the weather, but also to people who look to hurt them. Violence towards people experiencing homelessness has happened here recently, but hopefully our educational program helps to stop it in the future.

Once we had an idea of where we were going, we set off on foot to the first location. At first, I was nervous and didn't know what to expect. I thought that people would be mad when we woke them up, or try to harass us as we travelled down the street. There were some new people in our group and some

PIT Count veterans. The veterans wanted us to jump right in, so we began by waking people up who were sleeping in a parking garage. A couple of new people decided to leave because they said it was "unethical" to wake people up – they would rather just estimate the needed data (age, sex, ethnicity, veteran, etc.) – instead of disturbing their sleep. I was sympathetic to their feelings, but the reality is that the PIT Count does more than create a data set, it also helps outreach workers, such as PATH, create and sustain relationships with people. PATH works hard to get people into supportive housing, and when we woke people up, most of them knew the outreach workers already.

Abandoned properties are some of the most unsafe places to seek shelter.

Many of those who were awakened by our team were elated to see us. For one, we weren't there to tell them to move, or harass them in any way. They saw friendly faces who are connected to resources that can help them get through the winter. We would ask them to fill out their homelessness certification sheet. The sheet is basically an application for a VESTA Card, which is the ID card that individuals can use to access shelters, food banks, and other supportive services. By filling out the sheet with us that night, they are able to update their status and keep current with the system. This wouldn't happen if we let them sleep.

After we left the first parking garage, I was at ease and happy to lead the group through the neighborhood to each location. We met people who were having health crises and we were able to talk to them about where to get services. Others were happy to know that someone was checking on them. I just wish I was more prepared, (a few clipboards would have been helpful when filling out the forms and when taking the demographic data), so that things would have gone more smoothly. I learned that in the past, during the PIT Count, people have brought donuts and cookies, and I'm not sure if that's a good or bad thing. It seemed to go pretty smoothly without the food.

We came across an individual who had a motion detector set up around the sleeping spot. This person had only been experiencing homelessness for about two weeks and had never heard of PATH or even the Homeless Coalition. We spent a few extra minutes explaining what services are available, in terms of housing and health resources, before moving on. We combed through underpasses, wooded areas, and abandoned properties. By 2am, we were starting to lose steam, and we were wrapping up all the areas that were on our list. We went to a couple of places that weren't on the list, but I knew from living in the neighborhood. It felt good to add something to the process.

Stoops such as this may be someone's last resort.

I look forward to a time when these types of counts aren't necessary, but I am thankful we have such a strong Homeless Coalition in Cincinnati that stays on top of the issues while helping people access life-saving services. Even though it appears that HUD only requires this activity in January, on odd numbered years, I'm sure that we'll do it, not just for the numbers, but for the outreach opportunity.

SORRY NOT TODAY
04/06/2018

Whenever you pass someone on the street who is asking for help, what is your response? Do you stop to engage in a conversation? Do you have a quick one-line, like "Sorry, not today" or "God bless!" and keep walking? Do you reach into your pocket and find what change you might have? How we respond to panhandling is an important part of who we are. Our response is also a good indicator of what system of beliefs we hold.

We recently did a speaking engagement with a group of adults at a local church. We love speaking at churches because it usually means the congregation is taking homelessness, and the eradication of it, seriously. Typically, we'll meet after a service on Sunday, and give the speaker some time to tell their story, talk about solutions, and engage in questions. The questions can be very revealing.

At this church, the questions were coming one after another, but one question really stood out: "How do you know who is worthy of your donation? I mean - if I see someone panhandling, how do you decide if you'd give them money?" This question is not very unique, but the follow-up to our answer, we more telling than anything. The speaker, very succinctly, described the process of panhandling, the difficulties, the loss of self-respect, and the role of the passerby. If someone walking by makes eye-contact, and has a conversation, that is worth more than money at times. And the intent that you have, when you give someone a little change, is an intent of doing good... so let that intent be your purpose. Questioning how someone spends the money is actually very problematic.

The woman's response was very interesting. She said she goes to Findlay Market with her husband pretty regularly. And almost every time, someone asks them for change. She assured us that she and her husband are willing to give, but they have a test. The husband takes the hand of the person who is asking for money, and gives them a firm shake. If the hand is rough, she says, then the husband determines that the individual is willing to work and worthy of the donation, but if it's soft, he won't give them a dime. At that point, my heart sunk, and my mind started traveling in many directions: Why would someone do this? Is work a requirement for help? What if this is the first time someone had to ask for money? Who job is it to judge someone's worthiness? What is an appropriate response?

I quickly gained my composure and asked the speaker, who had panhandled, to give their perspective without attacking the method. Of course, the speaker was able to handle the situation, but it is something that stood out in my head for the past couple of months. What kind of society do we live in that demands that not only people look needy enough to be granted help, but also that calluses on hands are a determinant of someone's willingness to work? I have heard people say that if someone who is panhandling doesn't look homeless, then they won't give them any help. You do realize that most people who experience homelessness don't "look" homeless? That society's shame of homelessness creates a system where people work so hard to be not perceived as homeless? This is literally many people's daily goal — to get through the day without being looked down upon for their circumstance.

I guess it's hard to say what the appropriate response is in this situation. Yes, the husband doesn't ignore them, but he is still judging them. Being judged, whether you are without a home or not, is always a tough psychological situation to face. Once we break the dominant script around race, gender, sexual orientation, disability, or home status, it's very difficult to get that respect and understanding back. It's important for us to use our knowledge of homelessness (and the other fights in which we are engaged) to be advocates for all, no matter how society judges them (or us, for that matter).

NUMBER 1 OR NUMBER 2
06/01/2018

What's the first thing you do when you wake up in the morning? Chances are, you head straight into the bathroom to find some relief. Now imagine, you woke up today in an alley, or under a bridge. You still need relief, but where do you go?

Pick an alley. Look behind a bush. Your body is telling you it's time, but your surroundings are foreboding. Maybe I can hide behind this dumpster. Maybe not. In Ohio, public urination/defecation can result in a lifetime of issues. Although it's a misdemeanor, the resulting fine and possible jail-time, can stay on your record permanently. Failure to show up in court will result in a warrant, which sets the stage for more serious issues, including harassment by police.

The lack of public restrooms is a serious issue in Cincinnati. It doesn't take an investigator to find proof of this: alleyways smell of urine; piles of feces lay on the sidewalk; signs on bars read "No Public Restrooms" as if it's a campaign against restrooms altogether. A lack of readily available restrooms can lead to all kinds of health issues — from urinary tract infections, prostate issues, impacted colons, toxic shock syndrome — to the spread of bacteria and disease. This is a public health crisis.

Rarely do we consider how privileged we are to have a shower as well. Getting into the shower at the end of a long day, or to revive yourself in the morning, is something we take for granted. Consider missing those opportunities day-after-day, week-after-week, month-after-month, and you can see what kind of medical issues would pop up. Beyond body odor and matted hair and clothing, serious rashes, unclean sores, or wounds left untreated, will quickly chip away at your quality of life. Lack of public facilities to deal with these issues surely costs us more than providing them — so why do we fail so badly?

You can imagine my consternation when I learned that people have been "banned" from some of our remaining public restrooms by 3CDC employees. One or our speakers, from our speakers' bureau at the Homeless Coalition, told me a few months ago that Washington Park employees harassed them when they were leaving the bathroom. This individual sheepishly told me that they had to move their bowels, and once they finished, as they were leaving they were confronted by a park employee who accused them of "shooting up" in the bathroom and threatened to call the police. This speaker, who I have grown close to over the years and would have no reason to lie to me, was upset because they do not, nor have they ever used, IV drugs, as they are scared of needles. They were not shooting up in the bathroom, so from where did this baseless accusation stem?

Even more recently, I was approached by someone who I consider a neighbor, although they are experiencing homelessness in Over-the-Rhine. This person was visibly upset because they were "banned" from the Washington Park bathroom for allegedly "shooting up." While this person wasn't denying that they use IV drugs, they were mad because they, and others, have been accused of doing it in the bathroom when there is no proof. I asked if they knew if people had been "banned" from other 3CDC run public bathrooms — like Fountain Square, and they answered affirmatively. I spoke with a low-level 3CDC employee who said that they were in fact banning people from the bathrooms for drug use, even without visual proof that drug use was occurring. They said they have a camera in the foyer of the bathrooms, but not inside the bathrooms. This employee seemed to believe that banning people from using the bathroom was in their best interest, and would in fact stop people from using drugs altogether.

Anyone who has been following the heroin epidemic closely knows that

Due to lack of public bathrooms, a frequently used alley bathroom.

people are shooting up in more public places as part of a safety plan. If people overdose in private spaces alone, they are not very likely to get help, and could end up losing their life. We also know that sending people to jail for heroin use is also a death sentence, as one's tolerance drops while behind bars, and once released, the user injects the same amount as before, and quickly overdoses. This is why we will never police our way out of this particular health crisis.

What is going to take for the city to own up to its failures to provide decent basic services? Mayor John Cranley campaigned on providing basic public services, but absent in his promises were public restrooms, shower facilities, and even safe spaces for people to inject and exchange. Cranley lacks leadership qualities, vision, and compassion for people in our city who suffer the most — which clearly shows in his priorities. We must treat the health crisis seriously by providing 24/7 public restroom facilities (like Portland Loos), shower facilities, and safe, affordable housing for all who need it in our city. Let's not shut the door on our neighbors in need.

FAKING IT
06/01/2018

One question that we routinely receive is "how to tell if someone is faking homelessness." It's far too common of a question because it shows our lack of empathy and misunderstanding of homelessness. If we believe that even one person is faking it, will we fight hard for solutions? Mistrust is a difficult place to start, and perhaps, an even more difficult thing to change.

If you are making the decision to help someone, it is not unusual to want to know all the parameters before you decide to help. When a family member asks for assistance, sometimes you'll want to know all the details, and other times, you will just help, and not ask "how did you get in this situation?" or "can you prove to me that you need my help?" It's important to help people as you can, how you can, but it's even more important to help people in the way that they need help.

Short-term needs, like food, water, toiletries, can be helpful today — but they don't translate directly into housing for people who may be experiencing homelessness. Think where those items fit into the solutions to homelessness: Affordable Housing; Livable Wages; Tenant Protections. Although these solutions don't explicitly include toiletries, food, or water, they are necessary for everyday life.

My biggest issue with the idea of faking homelessness is the judgmental part. Typically, the topic comes up with panhandling, and whether we should give a dollar or two on the way to the ball game. As I have written before, some people come up with their own ways to determine if someone is worthy enough for their money. It could be based upon what they say, what their sign says, how they interact, the roughness of one's hands, or how shabby their clothes look. People will say "Well, you don't look homeless!" and keep walking. This type of judging doesn't allow for the many types of homelessness, including: homeless at home (not having food, water, electricity, support, etc. at home); doubled up (two families living together due to economic circumstance); couch surfing (staying at friends' and relatives' places); or living in a car (often showering at the gym). If you understand the types of homelessness, you'd realize that judging people by how they look will never be accurate.

Most people who experience homelessness work very hard to hide their circumstances. You wouldn't (or couldn't) tell by looking at them. This is mainly due to shame and social stigma. We are constantly bombarded with terminology and visual representations that convey the sentiment that people who don't have homes are not worthy participants in society. Just as they are trying to outlaw panhandling in Dayton, Ohio, we criminalize the lives of people who are already struggling to get by in a difficult world. Criminalizing homelessness actually causes and perpetuates homelessness by giving heavy fines, jail-time, and permanent records to people who are being marginalized by society. With all these systems trying to take you down, why would you want people to think you are experiencing homelessness?

There are several factors that go into trust, including whether someone is an expert, if they are consistent, if they are professional, and if they have some kind of altruistic intentions. People who experience homelessness should be trusted as experts. Their lived experience has weight to it. So, if you are unsure if someone is "faking it," why not ask them? Why not sit down and ask them to their face? Imagine doing this, and think about how it makes you feel — are you faking being a human who cares for people who are struggling? Or are you just a product of a capitalist society that favors profit over people and challenges the experiences of others?

WHAT CITY HALL GOT WRONG
07/22/2018

Last week, Cincinnati City Councilmembers, Tamaya Dennard and Chris Seelbach, requested a special public hearing regarding the imminent City eviction notices to people who are currently living under the Fort Washington Way Bridge (near Third Street, downtown). The session, hailed as an input session, turned out to be a way to postpone, but not indefinitely, the eviction until Wednesday, July 25th. At the beginning of the committee meeting, which then morphed into a special council meeting, it was announced by the city manager, Milton Dahoney, that an agreement had been reached between Bison (a self-appointed leader of the camp), Maslow's Army (Sam Landis, who has been assisting the campers), and the City of Cincinnati. The "solution" was to provide a portable restroom, a dumpster, and have a medical van come to the camp. None of the solutions included housing. Unfortunately, not only is the premise that eviction will "solve the problem" faulty, but there was other serious misinformation spread at the meeting as well.

First and foremost, the presumption that removing people from encampments will alleviate homelessness, is very wrong-headed. It will only displace the residents, pushing them further into the margins, and making them more likely to become victimized or physically attacked. It is not an ideal situation, living in the camp, but they have their own security measures and rules, including, a very strict drug-free expectation. Over and over again at the meeting, by councilmembers and the public, allusions to people experiencing homelessness as "dangerous" and "crime" were mentioned and fully asserted, even though the police themselves said there was no known crime associated with the camp. The unfortunate reality is, however, that people experiencing homelessness are much more likely to be victims of violent crime, rather than perpetrators of them. Pushing them further from the safety of the camp will not only cause psychological hardships, but also will create instability which generally leads to dangerous situations.

Throughout the week, the media sources made claims, just as they did after Ken Martin passed away in January, that shift the blame onto people who are experiencing homelessness, from the systems that marginalize and penalize people. For example, people at the City Hall meeting were shocked to hear that not everyone is allowed into the shelter system, and in fact, most are turned away because there just simply is no room in the shelter. If you know that more than 70% of the people who try to get into the shelter are turned away, would you have more understanding of why people are sleeping outside? While the winter shelter has less strict standards, there are some people who can never get into a shelter due to their past legal issues. We just can't believe that all people are worthy of shelter, food, and clothing, regardless of their history; nor, can we believe that someone who has "done the time" is able to put it in their past and move forward as a contributing member of society. Our country's reliance on criminal records to determine worthiness creates poverty, and should be examined and destroyed.

Even more disturbing, the City Manager put a local church, who had already made a statement saying they would not open as a shelter, in the plan without their consent. Prince of Peace Lutheran Church, which raises funds each year to run its own winter shelter in Over-the-Rhine, was asked to take in all of the campers but declined because they knew that it was a Band-Aid solution to a much bigger issue. They knew that if they opened their basement as a shelter for four weeks, it would be needed for two weeks more, and many weeks after that. Prince of Peace understands the systemic issues and the solutions to ending homelessness. Yet, the City Manager pressed that Prince of Peace was going to open the shelter, even though the church wasn't at the table during the last-minute agreement.

At the meeting, affordable housing, livable wages, and housing protections were only mentioned a few times. What this does is focus our energy on the 40 or so individuals who are living under the bridge, rather than the 40,000 units of affordable housing that are needed for families in the bottom of our county's annual median income (AMI). This is important because, as Councilmember Dennard claimed, if we don't deal with the systemic issues, we will find ourselves back here again having the same discussion. And the fact remains, everyone who asserted this statement is absolutely correct: just because you evict and erect a fence under a bridge, does not mean that you've solved anything, in fact, you are just causing more problems, when you don't create opportunity for affordable housing, livable wages, and housing protections. Many speakers were right to point out that this City Council has put housing in jeopardy in the West End through the FC Cincinnati Soccer Stadium Deal and tax abatements.

Finally, the face of homelessness in Cincinnati was never seen. The face of homelessness is a child of 9 years old, and no eviction could possibly help a child. The simple fact that the City's efforts to remove blight from under the bridge and Third Street is the main "solution" does not even being to address how most of the children in Cincinnati live in poverty, or how more than 75%

of African-American children in Cincinnati live in poverty, or how we have no upward mobility for people of color in our city. Evicting people and putting up fences, does absolutely nothing to solve a deep systemic issue — in fact, it makes it worse. The true solutions to the issue revolve around the City providing 24/7 bathrooms, with showers, access to city-funded health services, wage equity, public spaces, housing fairness, and fully funding the affordable housing trust fund. We know the solutions, but when will City Hall get it right?

CRUEL AND UNUSUAL PUNISHMENT
09/24/2018

When Common Pleas Court Judge, Robert P. Ruehlman, signed the motion filed by Hamilton County Prosecutor, Joe Deters, in agreement with the City of Cincinnati, at the behest of Mayor John Cranley, he effectively legalized cruel and unusual punishment for people who are experiencing homelessness. Building upon the already dubious, potentially illegal, restraining order which demanded that Cincinnati Police remove persons homeless from the public eye, the new motion expanded the reach into private property, including the encampment at the corner of 13th and Republic, in Over-the-Rhine. Today, the encampment has been moved, most persons dispersed to secluded areas, without a community to support them.

Throughout this entire ordeal, the City has maintained that there is "plenty of room" in the shelters to accommodate everyone at the site; however, City documents and personal accounts, including my own, have shown that there are not enough beds, and in fact, only overflow mats on the floor (sometimes on the laundry room floor) are available to select individuals. What seemed like a PR / funding move, the shelters bent over backwards to try to accommodate as many people as possible, sacrificing quality over quantity, and questioning whether the situation will be getting better or worse, during the upcoming winter months. The shelters are open 24 per day, 365 days a year, and work their hardest to not turn anyone away; however, some statistics show that more than 70% of people seeking shelter are turned away simply because there is not enough room.

Spending time on the streets, at the encampments, I was able to see firsthand how difficult it truly is to get shelter. I personally called 381-SAFE, the central access point line in Cincinnati, and sat on hold for over 25 minutes. After finally being able to talk to an operator, I was told that there were only 4 beds available (at the time, more than 40 people were in the encampment), 2 beds for youth, and 2 for men who have a job, or who are willing to work. By the time we made it to the men's shelter, the 2 beds were already taken. This gave the 62 year-old man I was working with little hope, and he is still out on the street today. Even as the police closed in on the camp, they expressed their frustration with the system, noting that they too could not get through, or if they had gotten through, there wasn't any available space.

Then there became another frustration, when people in the camp would be fast-tracked into housing, yet hundreds of people are languishing in the shelters already. People who heard they could get housing faster by staying at the camp began to show up, and while this is a good thing that people are having options, it also became frustrating when people who had moved four times with the camp, were still not getting connected to housing. We have been working with our member organizations, such as Lighthouse Youth Services and Over-the-Rhine Community Housing, to secure housing for as many people as possible. Every member of the Homeless Coalition staff has been actively involved in the housing process, and we've been actively trying to improve the process from the beginning.

Before the City and the County colluded to push forward the criminalization of homelessness at the State level, members of the camp had entered into a legal case at the Federal level, regarding the unconstitutionality of camp sweeps. It is seen as a Freedom of Speech issue, where tents represent the speech of persons who cannot access shelter or housing. The crux of the issue, as with the cruel and unusual punishment claim, is that there is no shelter or housing, and therefore, persons cannot be removed without a proper alternative. County Prosecutor, Joe Deters, admitted that the jail is also over-capacity, but said that people arrested for homelessness could "sleep on the gym floor," but did not elaborate on which gym, and if that would create more issues, rather than solving them.

In this whole debate, Cranley and Deters have been using stereotypes, rather than fact-finding to demonize people experiencing homelessness. They claim that everyone experiencing homelessness is a public health issue, that they are all drug abusers, and that they all have hepatitis A. However, other than one visit from the Health Department on 3rd Street, there has been no other health related outreach. People in the encampment said they were vaccinated against hepatitis with a single shot, but most vaccinations require multiple shots. They were unsure if they needed follow-up shots to complete their vaccination, and they were unsure if there would be any issues if they didn't receive follow-up shots. The funding for addiction services has also been called into question, as the Center for Addiction Treatment receives very little City funding, and what they do receive we have to fight for each year.

If the City wanted to end homelessness, they could with affordable housing, livable wages, and housing protections. If they want to cite health issues, then they could provide more health outreach, like mobile nurses, and easier access to health and addiction services. If this was a true health crisis, they would provide testing first, rather than blindly offer vaccinations. The issues that arise from homelessness should not be minimized, but they shouldn't be used as an excuse to punish people who are already suffering.

KNOW YOUR RIGHTS!
10/05/2019

Recently, the Homeless Coalition, in partnership with some of our member organizations, including Legal Aid and Housing Opportunities Made Equal (HOME), put on an information session at the Public Library of Cincinnati and Hamilton County's Main Branch. We created an informational session that would be useful to all as it focused on historical and contemporary issues, renters, homeowners, and landlords. We broke it into several pieces, starting with the history of homelessness in Cincinnati, the issues that we are currently fighting against, including displacement and criminalization, the basic laws that protect the rights of citizens, and ways to protect yourself from spurious landlords. Finally, we ended with ways to get involved, including hosting informational sessions, speakers, and joining us in our fight to eradicate homelessness.

The historical portion started with the 20th Century, and more specifically with redlining. The underpinnings of redlining include racism and classism, which essentially run current today. Redlining officially began after the Great Depression and exacerbated segregation in every city across America. A federal housing program forced people of color into substandard housing, while giving white people the ability to build generational wealth. Combined with legally enforced segregation and restrictive covenants, African-Americans were systematically denied the ability to create wealth through property ownership. After generations of racism in housing, we can certainly see the effects today on family wealth.

Following the Civil Rights Movement, when housing discrimination based on race was outlawed, people of color continue to be cut out of housing opportunities. As former President Reagan's policies of disinvestment in public housing decimated the quality of public housing, emphasis was put on religious institutions to create the safety net that people would need in a changing globalized economy. America began moving towards a service economy, which would push wealth to the very few. Reagan also perpetuated the myth that people "want to live outside" rather than viewing homelessness as a systemic issue. This began the era that we are currently in, of underfunding public housing while allowing it to deteriorate, and pushing money into private hands through programs like Section 8, which allow for private landlords to benefit from public money.

Although people believe that there are plenty of Section 8 housing vouchers out there, the window to apply only opens up every few years, for a few days. Some people who get on the waiting list will still be on the waiting list

3 or 4 years later, when the application period is opened again. The Cincinnati Metropolitan Housing Authority (CMHA) Section 8 Housing Choice Voucher waiting list is currently closed, it was last open for four days in January 2017; and before that in December 2014, and in 2012. Of all the low income renters in the United States, less than 25% who would be eligible for assistance actually receive it. This is occurring at a time when the cost of housing has risen, but wages have not. In Hamilton County, we are 40,000 units short of low-income housing for people making up to about $25,000. This means that people are living paycheck to paycheck, kids are sleeping on the floor, couches, sharing beds with infants, etc. Black residents are way more likely to be cost burdened in Cincinnati, while the average rent for an apartment in Cincinnati has skyrocketed to over $1100 per month.

Minimum wages do not cover the cost of a two bedroom apartment. The typical person who makes minimum wage is a 35 year-old woman with children. Her children cannot close the door and do their homework, or find a place to decompress after a difficult day because Mom can't afford a 2 or 3 bedroom apartment while public housing is full and Section 8 voucher waiting list is overburdened. She would have to work 104 hours per week to afford a 2 bedroom apartment on minimum wage. This is even more defined for Black families who are least likely to be home owners, as in 15-county Greater Cincinnati, homeownership rates are 74.5 percent for whites but 33.1 percent for Black families.

When it comes down the laws that should protect people who are experiencing homelessness, there are three main Constitutional Amendments that apply: First Amendment's protection of free speech; Fourth Amendment's protection against unreasonable searches and seizures; and the Eighth Amendment's protection against cruel and unusual punishment. Each of these protections has been recently violated by Hamilton County and the City of Cincinnati. Fortunately, the Homeless Coalition is currently fighting the criminalization of homelessness in Federal Court, and we continue to push for these rights while we continue to push for housing and housing protections. Finally, a healthy standard of living, including housing, is part of the United Nations' Declaration of Human Rights.

An update to the Criminalization survey was given, which showed that nearly half of all survey respondents (people currently experiencing homelessness) have been harassed by law enforcement officers, even when they were not breaking any laws. The goal of the survey is to push for a Bill of Rights, that will include the Right to Rest, the Right to Move, the Right to Housing, and other important human rights. This led into understanding current Tenant/Landlord Laws, including discrimination, retaliation, researching your landlord, eviction, and filing a complaint. HUD funded housing rights were also discussed, including the right of residents to have advocates, like community organizers, present at meetings and discussions about changes in housing. Creating tenant organizations was also discussed before ending on ways to get involved in the fight to eradicate homelessness: Affordable Housing, Livable Wages, and Housing Protections.

IT COULDN'T HAPPEN TO ME
10/11/2018

A common trope heard in advocacy circles is "It could happen to anyone." Whether we are talking about homelessness and hunger, or disease and sexual assault, there tends to be a moment where people's level of concern increases when they realize that it could happen to them, or someone close to them. In our work at the Homeless Coalition, we strive to uplift and amplify the stories of people who experienced homelessness so that the public can put a face on the issue. This humanizes an often distanced and muddied issue. Homelessness is a systemic issue, rather than a personal one, so this act is often confused as a "scared straight" tactic, even though the humanization of homelessness is what it will take to get people involved in the struggle for affordable housing, housing protections, and a livable wage.

Following a recent speaking engagement with the Homeless Coalition, one of the audience members said the event will stick out in their head because "It could happen to anyone." Each time I hear that, my heart sinks a little. The issue is really in that it erases historical and contemporary issues of equity, power, and control. Am I glad that people feel more strongly about the issue of homelessness because of this experience? Of course I am. But if you cannot see how the issue is related to structural violence, then your advocacy comes out of a place of selfishness, not out of a place of common decency, fairness, and equity.

Let's look at it through the lens of sexual assault. Could anyone be a victim of sexual assault? Of course. If you have a body or a mind, you can be victimized. But if 15% of women are raped, as compared to less than 3% of men, is it fair to erase the gender imbalance and say "Well, it could happen to anyone!"? That kind of mentality is not compassionate, nor is it realistic. It denies humanity to women who are deeply affected by this issue, and it doesn't allow for a full scope to be developed because underneath that one statistic there is a culture of violence against women. Women are likely to experience aggressive sexual acts on a daily basis, whereas men rarely are victims of sexual confrontations like catcalling, unwanted sexual advances, verbal harassment, stalking, etc.

The #MeToo movement was created by an African-American women because minority women are much more likely to be victims of sexual and violent crimes: Black women experience intimate partner violence at a rate 35% higher than white women. The movement was co-opted by the majority, effectively erasing the intersectionality of sexual violence. Gender, race, ethnicity, sexual orientation, gender identity, economic class, abilities, and even physical location, impact the likelihood and severity of sexual assault; therefore, saying "It can happen to anyone" erases those who are most vulnerable in our society.

This is also true for homelessness. Homelessness is growing for women and children at the highest rates, but for women who are Black, Native American, or Brown, the rates of homelessness (and poverty in general) are much higher than for white women. (There may be more white women living in poverty in the United States, but this represents a smaller percentage of white women than it does for Black women.) Black women in the United States will almost universally experience poverty either before or after their 65th birthday. This means their risk for homelessness, sexual assault, violent crime, adverse health, etc., are all disproportionately high. Saying "It could happen to anyone" ignores the structural issues that we do collectively have control over, and puts emphasis on individualism, which is messy and allows us to ignore the suffering by not acting.

In the end, your advocacy should be based on the simple notion of equity — that all people deserve to be treated with fairness — with the footnote that there is no universally applied remedy. The forces that create equity for one person, are not the same for everyone. The likelihood that something will happen to someone is wholly based on factors that were determined before birth, and have little to do with choices someone has made. Unless we accept the truth about structural violence, including racism, sexism, homophobia, xenophobia, etc., we will continue to hurt, and erase the lived experience of people who are victims of our unjust society, when we proclaim, "It could happen to anyone!"

UNDERREPORTED: OUT OF THE SHADOWS
11/07/2018

Homelessness is not just people sleeping on the street or in a shelter. When two families are living together due to economic necessity, it is called being "doubled-up," which is a form of homelessness. People living in their cars are experiencing homelessness. People who are couch-surfing, going from place to place, or just staying in the same place, are also experiencing homelessness. If you don't have food on the table and parental guidance, that's called being "homeless at home," which affects a great deal of school-aged children in our city. These are just some of the underreported types of homelessness that greatly affect our city today, whether it be concealed or in plain sight.

If your family is not on the lease, you are experiencing homelessness. Doubling-up is a common tactic that is used, generally within families, to help keep people off of the streets and out of shelters. Typically, doubling-up allows one family to bring in another while they try to work on their independence. In time, doubled-up families may face pressure from landlords, family members, school systems, and others to move out of the property. The family on the lease may decide they have had enough, and the other family is once again looking for options. Doubling-up isn't seen as a solution to homelessness because of the tenuous nature of the relationships that ensure stability.

After the new anti-homelessness laws were created this summer, people living in a car risk criminal charges in Hamilton County. Anyone who is found creating a "domicile" on public land is at risk for arrest. This may put pressure on PATH team members who are tasked with verifying the location of someone who is sleeping in their vehicle. The PATH team must see an individual or family sleeping outside, or in a vehicle, to grant them a homelessness certificate. This certificate grants them access to different services, including housing (when available), and is seen as the first step to getting off of the street. Strategies are developed when living in a vehicle, such as showering at the YMCA or the Mary Magdalen House, spending time at the Library to warm up, and trying to use the vehicle to make money through odd jobs. A couple of years ago, I wrote an article about a man who lost his foot to frostbite after sleeping in his car during the winter.

Couch-surfing is something that is relatively common among college-aged young adults, but people of all ages are forced into this category of homelessness. When someone has no place of their own, they often find refuge in the homes of their family or friends. Couch-surfers may try to give back by doing chores around the house, or keeping things cleaned up. There tends to be a time-limit to couch-surfing because people want their own space back or there are issues with the building management. Couch-surfers may lose their place on the couch when they are perceived as having nothing to give back for their presence. It is possible that someone may only couch-surf for a few days, but it probably would last a few months or more because securing stable housing is very difficult and time consuming.

When someone has a roof over their head, but no food on the table, or parents working all hours of the night, they are experiencing a type of homelessness. When they are sleeping on a couch or on the floor, this is another form of homelessness: homeless at home. When you understand that there is no place in the United States where someone who is making minimum wage can afford a two bedroom apartment, you realize that the children are sleeping on the couch and on the floor. They don't share dinners together, and often the only meal they receive is the one they get at school. Homeless at home is a place where hunger and homelessness meet, and where many of our youth are located in Cincinnati. More than 75% of African-American children in Cincinnati live below the poverty line due to pervasive racism, which means that most of them go without the food they need and they are battling homelessness in one form or another.

When we do the PIT Count in January, we are compiling data from shelters, supportive housing, and other institutions to create a number to represent the people who are experiencing homelessness in our city, county, state, and nation. We also join in teams to physically find and count people who are sleeping on the street, in doorways, under bridges, in woods, etc. These numbers go to the federal government to determine how much funding is needed to address the problem. Although we spend many hours on this endeavor, we only count people in 3 of Cincinnati's 52 neighborhoods. People who are doubled-up, couch-surfing, homeless at home, or living in their cars are almost completely left out of this count. The limitations of this one-night count are endless, even though we strive to include as many people as possible. Hopefully, this will make you cautious about any statistic you read about homelessness, and you know why people are under-counted when we are examining homelessness.

BOARDED UP
03/07/2019

How many people need to die on the street before we enact long-lasting systemic change? Last week, we honored the life of Danny Lee Miles, just 61 years old, on the corner of Race and Liberty. Danny Lee is just one of what will likely be over 100 people who die in Cincinnati because of homelessness in 2019. Every person who spoke at the memorial commented on how they wish they could have done more, that there is a crisis, and that Danny Lee was a kind and gentle soul. The details of his passing were unknown at the memorial, but we do know that he died alone, outside, in the cold, on a night with temperatures in the 20's.

The emotions on the corner ran high as clothing items and food were handed out to whoever needed them. Organizers, who want to honor Danny Lee, said that these items were being given out in honor of Danny Lee, from Danny Lee himself. Curious passersby, who stopped to ask what was going on, were shocked to learn of Danny Lee's passing, and many had stories to share about reaching out to him, and sharing food with him.

Danny Lee's life didn't need to end short. He had been living in a Northside group home for many years before finding himself out on the streets in October of 2018. A person connected with the group home said that he was de-comping, which means that his mental state wasn't able to handle stressors. This may have led him out to the street last fall, but the system ended up failing him. Several organizations and individuals had helped him while he was staying on the corner of Race and Liberty Streets, but ultimately, they were unable to prevent his death.

Danny Lee had been estranged from his family for almost two decades, but their communication with the organizers was similar to that of those who passed him by each day – they wish they had done more. It seems that his mental state had put up barriers between him and his family for some time. Although Danny Lee attended the University of Louisville and received an EMS Certificate, he was unable to care for himself at the end of his life. Some questioned if we could have forced him into the shelter, after all, Prince of Peace operates a winter shelter literally across the street.

Prayers, pleas, and calls for system change were the focus of the memorial. One family, who lives on the block, attended the memorial because they had brought him blankets, mittens, and other items over the past few months. The young kids looked on as their mother spoke, "...I even offered to get him an Uber to the homeless shelter one night because it was very cold. But he was like 'I'm okay, I'm okay.' You know that was the kind of person he was, he didn't ever ask for help, ever, but because we saw him every day, we wanted to help. It breaks my heart that we live in a city that would board up a doorway, to keep him from being seen on a main street, rather than give him the help that he needed. He was a human being. He was more than just a homeless face. He had a family. We loved him. We were his family."

3CDC's response to a death in the doorway was to board it up.

Danny Lee passed away in the doorway on Race Street, just out of sight from busy Liberty Street. He had been sleeping in the doorway on Liberty, but the doorway was recently boarded up. It seems clear that the purpose of the board was to prevent him from sleeping there, in the eyes of someone, to remove the blight. Since the doorways on Race Street, on the same building were not also boarded up, it seems clear that this was about visibility - they don't want people to see poverty in the gentrifying neighborhood. As "OTR" creeps northward into Over-the-Rhine and FC Cincinnati decimates the West End, only two blocks from where Danny Lee died, the push to remove signs of poverty have been elevated. But what does it mean to push people further into the shadows?

Liberty Street is literally a battleground right now. The City is back at the drawing board regarding the Liberty Street Pedestrian Safety initiative. The southern part of Over-the-Rhine may have a SID forced upon us, forcing affordable housing out of the area. North of Liberty, the Brewery District continues its plan to turn the neighborhood into a museum, erasing all contributions and existence of African Americans from the neighborhood. Liberty Street is a major traffic artery, with "rush hour" from 7am to 7pm during the weekdays, as it connects the two interstate highways. Those of us who cross Liberty daily know the dangers of the street, but dying, alone in the cold, is not on the agenda of any of these current battles.

A *Streetvibes* Distributor and Contributor made an impassioned plea for affordable housing at the memorial. She used her voice to bring light to the pressing issues that we face in the neighborhood today. At the podium, she proclaimed that "here in a city where developers are coming in, taking historical buildings, making them into storefront eateries, it's really heartbreaking... today people are buying these buildings, they are trying to genocize [sic]... move affordable housing out. The churches, the Homeless Coalition, and [the shelters], they are doing their part to try to help with affordable housing. The City of Cincinnati and City Council are to be ashamed of themselves to let this happen. City Council stand up, help your community - let's get affordable housing!"

We know how to eradicate homelessness through affordable housing, livable wages, and housing protections, but it seems to me that people are still stuck in the mentality that it's the fault of the individual, so therefore we have no responsibility. This mentality can be traced back to the Reagan Administration, who pushed the idea that churches should be responsible for dealing with homelessness, not the government. Unfortunately, the government has manufactured the current housing and homelessness crisis. By dismantling public housing in favor of privatization, by rewarding developers for displacing residents in favor of market-rate housing, by allowing wages to fall way below a livable wage, by giving landlords carte blanche protections to deny and remove people from housing, the government has created and maintained a system that has resulted in the crisis we have today.

We have been to too many funerals over the past few years. The Homeless Coalition's memorial service that takes place on the longest night of the year counted over 110 people last year who died due to homelessness. Over the past year, the City and County have worked together to make it an arrestable offense to live outside on public or private property. The claim that people who are living outside pose a significant threat to the public is wrong, and forces people further into the shadows, further into isolation. Here we have an individual who was seen every day, yet was in danger himself, and the system wasn't enough. We are short 40,000 units of affordable housing. All the shelters are over capacity.

The jail is also overcrowded. Unless we do a major affordable housing push, a push for livable wages, a push for housing protections, the number of people who lose their lives to homelessness will continue to rise.

While so many people are gaining from the displacement of people from our neighborhood, shouldn't they take on some of the burden? We've lost more than 2400 units of affordable housing in Over-the-Rhine over the past 10 years. We are hemorrhaging our neighbors, yet someone is making a great profit off of it, using benefits and public incentives that come out of our taxes. The family who helped Danny Lee with blankets and mittens and offered to get an Uber to the shelter ended their memorial statement with this call to action. "We live on a block with all these vacant buildings. No one's doing anything with them but making a profit eventually… we have to do better as a people. We just got to do better. No one should have to die outside, alone, in the cold."

UNDER THE LAW
05/02/2019

"Why don't the people with too much money help the people who are struggling to get out of poverty?" This is the question that a middle-schooler asked me after an Over-the-Rhine People's Movement Walking Tour this week. The student had just been exposed to the real history of our neighborhood and was noticing the stark contrasts between the rich and the rest of us. Noting the number of BMW's that were parked on each block, the student was confused as to how people would just ignore suffering around them as they sauntered into bars and restaurants, trying to ignore the people holding signs and asking for help. The middle school student pointed it out on every block between 12th and 14th Streets, along Vine Street. Wealth and income inequality are so pervasive in the United States right now, that some have said it hasn't been this bad since before the Great Depression.

Our walking tours provide people with a perspective that is purposefully left out of the other walking tours in the neighborhood. After yesterday's tour with the middle school students, one of the chaperones pulled me aside to thank me for starting off with the Native American presence in the area. She told me that "most people just don't even care about the destruction of Native American communities... they just act like they never existed." While this is something that I understand to be true, it made me connect the dots between the person who is denial about wealth inequality who just parked his BMW and scuttled into a boutique on Vine Street and the people who believe the earth is flat, or that vaccines cause autism, or that climate change is not the fault of humans. All of these people have one thing in common – their inability to look directly at facts and accept them. But the facts behind wealth inequality reveal something even deeper about the American psyche.

Wealth inequality has been an obvious characteristic of American from day one, when the wealthiest man in America was elected our first President and the people who were tabulated as his wealth, people from Africa who were enslaved, had absolutely nothing other than some fictionalized debt to pay to America's founding. African-Americans have always been held back by white people in this country through laws and practices. The laws, or de jure, have been crafted to keep Black people from obtaining and retaining wealth. Laws such as slavery in the south, and the Black Codes in the north, gave way to a legal process in which Black people are exploited for their labor, ideas, innovations, and companionship. Black Codes in Ohio required all African American people who desired to live in Ohio to have two white people vouch for them at a courthouse and pay a large sum of money. The state of Ohio was literally built using these funds, as the law went into effect within a year of statehood.

Other northern states, such as Illinois, also used laws to make it legal to sell the labor of African Americans who were otherwise residing in a "free state." These laws continued through the end of slavery and into the Jim Crow era. Jim Crow was marked by segregation and laws that kept African-Americans out of the housing market and forced them into segregated communities that were disinvested in for decades. The ability to create generational wealth, that was given by federal policies to white people, was forbidden by law for Black people. These laws didn't end with the era of Jim Crow, they were just replaced by the era of mass incarceration, in which we currently reside. America has never been meritocracy, and we have never had a level playing field.

At a speaking engagement this week, we heard from Melissa who shares her story of homelessness, that basically lasted the first 50 years of her life. She discusses her journey to her first apartment, including times of isolation and loneliness that come from homelessness. With the rise of criminalization of homelessness, we are indeed seeing more de jure implications for people experiencing homelessness. When Melissa slept on the sidewalk before she found housing, it wasn't illegal to do so, but today it is different. Last year, Mayor John Cranley and County Prosecutor Joe Deters made it illegal to experience homelessness in all of Hamilton County, on public or private land. When the police and sheriff started to enforce this law, real people were hurt. One man had a heart-attack when they came to sweep his tent off of Third Street. Another man jumped off a bridge into the Ohio River. A young woman was interrogated by the police at the encampment near the Casino and walked off before her ride to the youth shelter arrived. She had no shoes, and was possibly being sex-trafficked, but the network of people that was assembled to help her had not arrived before she was scared off by the police, never to be seen again. These laws have had a direct impact on the lives of people who are struggling to get help in a city where most people are turned away from shelter and the lack of affordable housing is literally sending more than 100 people to an early grave each year.

Another kind of discrimination that occurs without the direct application of laws, is what is called de facto, which occurs because of market and social trends. When real estate agents direct potential buyers into certain neighborhoods, this is a form of de facto segregation. When parents choose specific schools based upon their racial makeup, or when people choose churches with people who are of their "own race," these are forms of social control that advocate for segregation, for a social hierarchy. De facto segregation is occurring every day. I need to be clear that while blockbusting was used to lower prices in white segregated communities, there is a new type of blockbusting occurring in our inner-ring neighborhoods, where Black people are simultaneously seeing their property taxes go up, yet the sale value of their homes is going down. It is not a success when a neighborhood becomes more "diverse" if the power of the minority groups is non-existent.

Melissa also spoke to the group about how she is housing insecure because of the proposed FC Cincinnati soccer stadium project. She has been living in the West End for a couple of years now, becoming more active in the community. She sees her friends receiving eviction notices directly from FC Cincinnati's property manager, and she is worried that her home will be next. FC Cincinnati commissioned a housing report to be released this summer that already shows that 53% of the West End residents are likely to lose their housing in the next 5 years. Imagine if someone told you that half of your neighbors would be gone in 5 years, how would you feel about your neighborhood? The forces of displacement have been ignited by the proposed soccer stadium, yet the team refuses to take responsibility for it, as Jeff Berding, team spokesperson, claims that they have not committed any crimes. Well, that's a low bar, don't you think? When we know that de facto segregation, discrimination, racism, etc., occurs on a daily basis, we'd hope to have higher standards for a project that is receiving millions in city tax-payer subsidy.

When we think about the middle-school perspective of what is right and just, it's hard to understand why we allow the millionaire class to make the laws, enforce the laws, feel they are above the law, while everyone else suffers under the law. Criminalizing homelessness is not the answer, but perhaps we should criminalize those who make people homeless, like the real estate lobby, the landlords, the developers who throw entire communities out on the street, the bankers who still redline, the politicians who allow for the illegal funding of our schools, the healthcare systems that function for profit, the polluters and carbon emitters who are at fault for global warming, and the fossil fuel industry that killed public transportation. Let's first start by taking away the subsidies for luxury development and soccer stadiums, and focus our budget on the lack of affordable housing in our county and city. We will never have enough money to satiate the rich, but we do have enough to ensure everyone has a safe and affordable place to live.

DOUBLE STANDARDS
08/08/2019

Through phrases like "Judge not, lest ye be judged," "People in glass houses shouldn't throw stones," and "Treat others how you would want to be treated," we may be taught at an early age that judging people is wrong. When it comes to homelessness and poverty, the judgements are often part of mainstream American culture as well. Stereotypes of laziness, dirty, drug addicted, mentally ill, and uneducated people are often weaponized against people in poverty, as well as people from particular neighborhoods or regions. Appalachian people are characterized as poor even though their labor and resources continue to be exploited. Black communities are at a decidedly large disadvantage and portrayed as lazy and incapable, even before birth, yet our country's wealth was literally built from the labor of Black people who were enslaved for hundreds of years. The stereotypes not only mischaracterize whole groups of people, but they say more about the people who hold them in their heads than anything else.

The Homeless Coalition's Education Program offers a series of events and activities to break down stereotypes and to instill an understanding of homelessness. We do this because a better informed public is more able and willing to fight injustice, such as the criminalization of homelessness, with the information and experience they gain through our programs. We have been working with schools, community groups, churches, and others to help gain a firm understanding of the issues facing the people experiencing homelessness and our responsibility as active citizens. The issue of Double Standards came up again last week, and it is worth examining it further.

During a *Streetvibes* Shadow Activity, where a *Streetvibes* Distributor (in this case, Lee McCoy) tells the group about themselves, *Streetvibes*, the program's values, and the City's Anti-Solicitation Ordinance, participants are equipped with a pitch and they are able to go into the streets to try to distribute the paper. As a controlled panhandling experience, participants witness many things, including people ignoring them as they walk by. Last week, one of the youth was convinced that a businessman, who said he had no money to donate, was lying to him. As the youth was telling the story, he quickly said, "but it's ok, because he was in a hurry anyway," which made me question the double standard that we have regarding people experiencing homelessness who fly a sign and panhandle, who, by and large, are accused of lying about their need, their use of the money received, even if they are actually experiencing homelessness. The student quickly excused the businessman for lying, so why do we hold other people to a higher standard, especially when they have less resources to uphold the standard?

Hearing from our Speakers, like Cleo, Sam, Willa, and Melissa, you can see how double standards created difficult circumstances in their lives. When you are being put in a box by society even when you try so hard to break out, the notion of becoming your true authentic self is challenged by people around you that are judging you for your past, rather than your current work. The work ethic of each of the speakers during their homelessness was far greater than what someone who inherits their wealth is likely to pursue. Just trying to figure out where to sleep, bath, eat, or get work requires a severely high level of commitment and hustle. Yet, people experiencing homelessness are routinely judged as lazy, even though most men experiencing homelessness have a job – the wages are too low to sustain a high standard of living.

On our walking tours, we see Double Standards in action where fancy restaurants are able to take half of the sidewalk for outdoor seating. The permanent barriers are required for alcohol sales and consumption on the sidewalk. A person works a hard day and then wants to relax with a beer, if they can afford to do it in their home or get a craft brew at a fancy restaurant, they can do it on the sidewalk. But if they are experiencing homelessness and sitting on a stoop, they could be criminalized for that. The same double standard is seen in Washington Park, which has a liquor license and several craft beers from which to choose. If you bring in a bagged beer from the store, you may be hassled or fined for bringing it into the park. Is this Double Standard fair and just?

People often wrongly believe that drug addiction and mental illness are the main causes of homelessness. This enables us to feel better about society's failures, and our desire to not help people. What is even worse is that drug addiction and mental illness are not the fault of the individual who is suffering, so even if these were the causes of homelessness, more compassion, not a turned back are what would be needed. Since homelessness is a result of policy decisions about housing, wages, and civil rights, we need to seek justice in these areas, rather than focusing on what an individual experiencing homelessness can do to change their current condition. Drug addiction and mental illness are often caused by homelessness, so we need to expand our rapid rehousing programs along with affordable housing, livable wages, and housing protections to reduce homelessness in our region.

While it may be easy for us to judge in our society, we must remember to move past the Golden Rule, which I cited above, and move to the Platinum Rule: "Do unto others as they would have you do unto them, not as you would have them do unto you." We can't just rely on our own values to craft how we interact with the world – we must ascertain and use the wishes and values of others to create a world in which everyone is valued, regardless of our own personal worldview. In that world, the Double Standards fade to the back, and we are able to see people as who they are, not what they represent to us.

CRIMINALIZATION OF EXISTENCE
09/16/2019

Last night, as I was preparing dinner, I heard police sirens outside of my window. My neighbors were celebrating a birthday behind their building, away from the street – dancing, playing cards, socializing, and watching the children play. It was a joyous occasion, with Stevie Wonder's birthday tribute to the Reverend Dr. Martin Luther King Jr. playing over the speaker. The police cruiser's lights created a sort of disco atmosphere along Republic Street, and the party turned the music down briefly. Shouts of "Fuck the police" start to fill the air, and the music goes back on. The police officer tries to reason with them, "Could you please turn the music down?" and the party continues. Moments later, a neighbor from another building goes to throw their trash away, less than three feet from the police cruiser, my muscles tense up. What if they decide to take it out on this random neighbor?

    The police cruiser moves a couple of times during these few tense moments, and eventually heads down Republic while the party continues. Did someone complain about the music, or did the police, who have a constant presence on Republic Street, take it upon themselves to try to break up the party? At 8pm? On a Sunday? All of the sudden, a simple party becomes criminalized and the relations between the police and the citizens become strained. Eventually, the police come back and enter private property to force them to end the party.

    The criminalization of existence has been a common thread in American history. Obvious examples include the institution of slavery followed by Black Codes, Jim Crow, and Mass Incarceration. Anti-sodomy laws that were unlawfully only applied to people in certain relationships, and the criminalization of the Islamic Faith that is seen at airports and traffic stops across the country, are other ways in which someone's identity has been criminalized in this country. We also see this with homelessness — whereas people who are only trying to survive, are thrown into jail, even just briefly, to create a criminal record. And with the 13th Amendment's loophole on slavery, we continue to enslave people in our prisons, even making your license plate for 21 cents an hour.

    We currently have a unique criminalization occurring across our country as people of Hispanic and Latino backgrounds are being criminalized and even stripped of their citizenship. Changes in the way the government is structured, stemming from the beginning of the War on Terror, have made it easier for the government to criminalize the existence of people who contribute massively to our country, while leaving them unsure of their future status here.

Just like in gentrification, where the two types, direct and indirect, destabilize a community, we have a destabilization of the Hispanic and Latino communities. People are being directly deported, having their citizenship called into question, and even recently starting to revoke birth certificates of people born near the border of Mexico, before deporting them to a country they never knew. People are also being indirectly terrorized, wondering what the future looks like, and if the future in this country is even plausible, as the social network is broken down.

Indirect gentrification erodes the social connections that someone has in their community – all of the things that make it their community are gone, so why stay here? When your family and friends have been deported, when the industries are forced to go underground, and the threat of ICE looms over you every day, why would you try to stay in this place, whether you are a citizen or not? The massive loss this represents to all Americans in the States may never be quantified in monetary terms, but the loss it represents for our culture is shocking.

It is said that people from Mexico did not cross the border, but the border crossed them. When the US stole the land from Mexico, people had been living there for thousands of years. We imposed new cultures and ideals upon the people living there without their consent. It was done by force. And today, we continue to use force through ICE and the police to impose certain values, certain middle class white values, upon the many cultures that exist in the country. The problem is, no matter how hard you push your white middle class values on people in non-white communities, they will never become white. White supremacy, even as fallacious as it is, ensures a certain type of inequity that cannot be reduced in a capitalistic world where certain needed labor is undervalued, and labor that serves only the wealthy is privileged. A permanent economic underclass is ensured by a police state.

Now, ICE is claiming that they don't need warrants to enter people's homes, and that they are authorized to violate certain civil rights. Isn't it ironic that an organization, ICE, that was created less than 20 years ago, is able to shirk civil rights laws and act like a terrorist organization themselves. In the War on Terror, ICE has become the chief mechanism of creating terror in the United States. Anywhere that is near any border, ICE has stepped up its raids and reign of terror. Even as close as Columbus, Ohio, ICE is operating random searches. Even as close as Butler County and Burlington Kentucky, ICE has detention facilities which coordinate with local agencies, such as the Hamilton County Sheriff. There is another ICE office in Blue Ash, just minutes from Cincinnati.

No matter what you feel about immigration, the very thing on which America was built, you have to question if the creation of Homeland Security and ICE (as it functions today) has been an appropriate response to the events of September 11, 2001. Have the massive deportations under the Obama administration, the family separation under the Trump administration, the stripping of citizenship for only non-white citizens, made you and your family safer? Even more pressing, has it decreased or increased the likelihood of terrorism, the main enemy in the so-called War on Terror? As with most criminalization, it does nothing but create barriers for people who are otherwise trying to live an honest life in a totally dishonest system.

I DIDN'T EVEN KNOW
09/30/2019

Homelessness may seem like a complicated issue, and for the most part it can be. While experiencing homelessness, daily tasks such as showering, eating, and working can be daunting tasks. The isolation, loneliness, and depression that comes with homelessness leads to greater likelihood of drug abuse, risky sexual activity, mental stress and illness, as well as, suicide. The experience of homelessness will likely follow you for the rest of your life, lowering your life expectancy. In Cincinnati last year, more than 120 people died from homelessness, with an average age of 51. These are only the people we were able to account for, as with all statistics around homelessness, the numbers are always lower than reality.

Have you considered where you'd register to vote, if you're experiencing homelessness? Ohio law says that your home is any place you intend to return to. People can use park benches as their address, but they won't get their mail delivered to a park bench, so they will not be able to participate in the voting process (as there are required documents that need to be mailed). Being able to get mail on a regular basis is a luxury that many people, in all types of homelessness, are not able to enjoy.

In Hamilton County, more than 25,000 people will experience homelessness this year. Less than half of those people will come in contact with the Homeless Management Information System (HMIS) that reports back to the federal government on the severity and need surrounding homelessness. National data has shown that less than 25% of people who are eligible for housing support actually receive it. And with a deficit of more than 40,000 units of affordable housing, Hamilton County is in a housing crisis. More than 10% of Cincinnati Public School students will experience homelessness this year, meaning they have no stable housing, or they will lose their housing at some point during the school year.

The homelessness crisis is real, and it affects everyone, regardless of your housing status or income level. When people learn the types of homelessness, they often remark that they didn't realize that they had experienced, or are currently experiencing homelessness. It is often jarring to realize that the support that you thought you had actually kept you on the edge of homelessness, or that your idea of what a "home" is has to be reevaluated. From couch-surfing to sleeping rough, homelessness has a negative effect on the individual and community.

Couch surfing is often seen as a rite of passage after major events, like graduation, or even just during summer break from school. But more often, adults who are not in school, are spending time on their friends' and families' couches. Trying to help out where they can by cleaning out the garage, babysitting, taking care of the yard, or helping to pay a portion of the energy bill. This type of homelessness is difficult to get out of because people end up spending a lot of their time and energy trying to please friends and family, so getting on their own two feet becomes impossible with the lack of time to spend on seeking out independence. Even if someone is sleeping on a bed, they are couch surfing. Couch surfing is not considered homelessness in some models and is often overlooked like doubling up.

Doubling up is when two families are living together out of economic necessity. Once again, this could be living with friends or family, and is very similar to couch surfing. Only one family has their name on the lease and is legally allowed to occupy the home. Many times family members double up so much that they think it is a normal way of life, not realizing that it is a form of homelessness. Because there is no place in the United States that a minimum-wage worker can afford a two bedroom apartment, many times the working poor are doubled up, even while working full time. The wages don't allow for families to become independent, while leaving families vulnerable to eviction or abuse.

Sometimes, after exhausting couch surfing opportunities, people find themselves sleeping in their cars. Afterall, homelessness is an economic issue, not a moral one. If it was a moral issue, we would not let it happen, but because it is an economic issue we are able to continually justify homelessness. There is an entire reddit devoted to car-habitation and how to modify your vehicle so that it is more comfortable to live in. Readers exchange tips on how to find safer parking spots, prepare food in your car, and create the most comfortable sleeping situation. Imagine keeping all of your possessions in your car and sleeping in it every day. Where will you shower? How will you get a hot meal? This car might be the last thing someone owns, and they may be about to lose it to repossession or citations.

Last year, Cincinnati saw a standoff regarding the street encampments. Ultimately, the City and County colluded to make it illegal to experience homelessness on private or public land in the entire county. While this puts more than 25,000 vulnerable people into an even more stressful and dangerous situation, it does nothing to end homelessness. The Homeless Ban has forced people further into the shadows, putting them at considerable risk. People who sleep on the street have a right to under the First, Fourth, and Eighth Amendments to the United States Constitution to do so. While this is being settled in federal court, understanding that it is not desirable to live outside, even with a tent, but it is difficult, dangerous, and leads to poor health outcomes, can help us come up with create and humane ways to reduce homelessness.

If you are living in a motel, that is a type of homelessness. Motels are only designed for brief stays, and living in one room with a small refrigerator and a contraband hotplate, while it may seem better than living in a tent, will result in lowered health outcomes as well. Eating fried, cheap food, sleeping many people in one bed, having nowhere to decompress, paying most of your income on just a room, will lead to long-lasting physical, emotional, and psychological harm. Families need stability and the ability to be a part of a specific community, which cannot be done while living in a motel.

Homeless at home is another type of homelessness that affects countless people in our region. The number of people who experience this type of homelessness isn't included in the 25,000 people who will experience homelessness this year in Hamilton County but it also has a very negative effect on our community. Many youth especially experience this type of homelessness where they have a roof over their head, but there is no food on the table or parental guidance. Children are often receiving their only meals at school or going to a neighbor's house for something to eat.

If you're paying more than 30% of your income towards your housing, you may just be a paycheck away from losing it all. Most Americans don't have at least $1000 in savings, leaving us closer to homelessness than ever. Even if you are getting in a relationship for a place to stay, this is still a form of homelessness until you have a lease in your name. People who are vulnerable to homelessness include people who have experienced homelessness throughout their lives. The wealth gap created by race-based policies that lead to white generational wealth has given us a system where Black people are way more likely to experience homelessness. Unless we have a restructuring of wealth with an eye on race in this country, homelessness will continue to rise, creating with it new types of homelessness that fall beneath the radar and certainly don't make it into any governmental count. Educate your friends and families on homelessness so that they can work harder to create a more stable and equitable community.

AN ALTERED STATE OF HOMELESSNESS
10/31/2019

Recently, the Council of Economic Advisers, an agency within the Executive Office of the President, released a document entitled The State of Homelessness in America. The document attempts to provide information about the problem of homelessness, as well as, the solutions to reducing homelessness. We have seen many reports on homelessness and poverty throughout the years, but I felt compelled to address this one because it has the potential to cause severe harm throughout the country.

Police officers follow instructions to remove people and tents from public space.

The document begins by stating the causes of homelessness in America. We know that the lack of affordable housing, the lack of livable wages, and the lack of housing protections all contribute greatly to homelessness. Each of these aspects are connected, as if someone has a larger income, they would be able to afford more for housing. The document does say, in the Executive Summary, that incomes do contribute to the inability to afford housing; however, none of the remedies address this cause, and it is not explored in detail in the study. The causes that are given are largely based on stereotypes and aren't consistent with a nuanced understanding of the issues surrounding poverty.

In this document, good weather becomes a catalyst for homelessness. The idea that people are choosing to live outside is a dangerous fallacy. People do not wish to live outside where they are more likely to experience adverse health outcomes, harassment, and violent crime. To blame the weather on homelessness is like blaming the moon for nighttime. It is far-fetched and disconnected from reality. There was no discussion on how to address the good weather aspect of homelessness either, although we do know that climate change will continue to increase homelessness, and as the earth warms, inhabitable areas of the planet will continue to increase.

At a Housing Now! rally, a list of names of people who have died early due to homelessness is presented to the city.

The study also blames high quality, hygienic, shelters for homelessness. The belief that people are leaving their safe and affordable homes to live in shelters is faulty at best, dangerous at worst. Some areas have a Right to Shelter law, which means that people who show up, shelter must be provided in a reasonable manner. The document says that these laws raise the quality of the shelters which makes them more desirable; thus, attracting people from their homes into shelters.

On top of good weather and high quality shelters, according to the document, people are experiencing homelessness because it is too desirable to live on the street. The document says that people are leaving their safe and affordable homes to live outdoors because municipalities have become too soft on people seeking shelter on the street. In cities, like Cincinnati, we have criminalized homelessness through our anti-solicitation laws, our encampment laws, and now Hamilton County's anti-homelessness laws. The last law, the county-wide law, allows the police to arrest anyone, on private or public land, who they suspect is experiencing homelessness. This law has not decreased homelessness, but it has made it more dangerous for people who are experiencing homelessness, especially for Black people who are more likely to be brutalized by the police, jailed unlawfully, and suffer long-term economic issues related to the criminalization of homelessness.

The document goes to further stigmatize homelessness by relying on an out-of-date stereotype that mental illness causes homelessness. While some people may experience homelessness due to mental illness, it is because they aren't able to access the proper support to remain housed. We also know that the trauma related to the experience of homelessness stays with an individual for their entire life. The trauma of not knowing where you'll sleep, and what you may have to give up of yourself to rest, can begin to affect your brain functioning within hours of experiencing homelessness. Other typical tasks, such as eating and bathing, become an emotional and physical challenge, further increasing trauma. Not to mention interactions with institutions who are meant to help, but instead deny you aid, that exacerbate suffering.

Scapegoating drug users as the cause of homelessness, as this document does, is also a fallacy. The causes of drug addiction are depression, isolation, and loneliness. A person who experiences homelessness will experience each of these risk factors, which may contribute to drug use. Drug use itself, however, is rarely a cause of homelessness. Blaming drug abuse and mental illness is a way to detract from the actual causes of homelessness by making it seem like a person has made the wrong choices, or they themselves are immoral. Addressing these issues is practical, but it is only addressing a symptom of a larger issue.

The document goes on to obfuscate the issue by presenting economic models that may have been ripped out of an introductory economics textbook. The discussion on the graphs amounted to the idea that housing costs too much to produce, so therefore, if we reduce the cost of production, then the rents will drop. This became the tactic to end homelessness: deregulation. The document presents deregulation as the main solution to ending homelessness. They believe that removing building codes, permits, environmental, housing, and wetland protections, combined with reducing energy efficiency and labor requirements, that the cost of housing would decrease so much, that in a city like San Francisco, rent would drop 55%, leading to a drop in homelessness by 54%.

The quality of housing is not considered in this model. Safety is not considered in a model that removes building codes and other protections. In fact, this plan may actually increase homelessness by permitting building in floodplains, reducing labor standards, and reducing the need for inspections and building trades, among other issues.

While it's hard to stomach the narrative that is created in this document, it is worth taking some time to digest. The final parts of the document make the claim that homelessness is increasing, and any count is not going to be accurate. This was, in my opinion, the only accurate part of the document, but it was only done to say that the Obama Administration failed when it comes to homelessness — it was a jab at President Obama.

Overall, the document relies heavily on stereotypes, in terms of the causes of homelessness, and it only relies on boot-strap approaches to ending homelessness. The major solutions that they propose are dangerous and will increase homelessness. The document says that the police should be supported in their brutality against people experiencing homelessness. The document says that building codes and other community safety considerations (environmental, for instance) are too costly and should be removed. It says that rent control also increases homelessness, but does not address or illustrate how it is a cause of homelessness. Like much of the document, it is based upon beliefs, so that it can put the solution on the individual (who needs drug rehab and mental services) rather than on an economic system that ensures income and wealth inequality.

ACTIVITY

Tactics of Gentrification: Photographic Neighborhood Assessment

Directions: Please read all the directions before beginning. This Neighborhood Assessment can be used in a variety of ways and in any location. The focus of the assessment is gentrification. This assessment asks participants to take pictures within a neighborhood to amplify the ways in which gentrification affects residents. Each part contains several items to document with your camera. <u>Underlined items MUST be documented.</u> Participants then may choose an additional three (3) items from each part to document. Participants may choose to document more than the required number of items. (Alternatively, groups could be assigned a part.)

While this event may elicit certain feelings of excitement, this should not be used to create a game or amusement of the effects of gentrification on residents. Please make sure you are respectful in every aspect of your conduct. **Use the Glossary if you have questions or need clarification on any of the concepts. For more background information regarding these concepts, please refer to the following articles: The Allure of Gentrification, Hostile Design, and Do You Speak Like a Gentrifier. Also, see Study Questions for reflection questions for this activity.**

Part 1: Senses

<u>We use our senses to gather information about the neighborhood. Document locations, items, and people that impact our senses to highlight cultural aspects in the community.</u>

Hear

See

Touch

Taste

Smell

Part 2: Community Ties

Find an example of an item that honors the life/legacy of another person.

Find an example of an economic or social issue, such as homelessness, hunger, or illness.

Find something that attempts to address that issue.

Ask someone for directions.

Find something that shows gratitude.

Find an example of coded language.

Find a menu 'out of reach' of a typical neighborhood resident.

Find an open public restroom.

Part 3: Hostile Design

Find 3 examples of hostile design.

Find a security camera in a public space.

Find a security sign.

Find an example of a publicly accessible space that cannot be fully accessed.

Find a gated off alleyway.

Part 4: Policy Focus

<u>Find the use of public space for private gain.</u>

Find an instance where business interests are favored over resident's interests.

Find an example of promoting minority entrepreneurship.

Find examples of crumbling infrastructure.

Find evidence of police presence.

Part 5: Community Change

<u>Find an example of disinvestment next to an example of investment. (Contrast)</u>

Find something that has been renamed.

Find a recently closed-down business.

Find a culturally-specific business/restaurant that is considered trendy right now.

Find a dog park or a pure-bred dog.

Find a brewery.

Find a sidewalk narrowed by business interests.

Bonus: Use https://www.hamiltoncountyauditor.org/ to find the **owner** of the property at 1305 Walnut.

GLOSSARY

Affordable Housing: Affordable means that a household is paying no more than 30% of their income towards their housing, including utilities. On a community level, housing is considered affordable when it is affordable to families making 60% AMI or less. In Cincinnati in 2020, 60% AMI would represent households making approximately $35,000 per year. Additionally, 30% AMI is approximately the wage for a fulltime minimum wage earner, or about $15,000 per year.

Area Median Income (AMI): If all households are lined up from least income to most income, the household in the middle is 100% AMI. Half of the households make more than 100% AMI, while the other half of the households make less than 100% AMI.

Black Codes: Laws restricting Black residents. In Ohio, for instance, these laws began when Ohio became a state, and lasted nearly until the Civil War. For decades, these laws prohibited Black residents from owning land, attending schools, owning guns, or representation in courts, but required Black residents to pay a fine upon arriving in Ohio and fines each year for all the members of the Black families.

Cincinnati Center City Development Corporation (3CDC): A private non-profit organization whose board is chosen by the mayor of Cincinnati, and whose membership includes large corporations and firms. 3CDC has many streams of revenue and is responsible for the Downtown and the Over-the-Rhine South Special Improvement Districts (SID). 3CDC has been referred to as the "preferred developer" by the city, yet no designation exists in the city's charter. 3CDC aggressively pursues public funding and tax credits to fund their projects. In general, 3CDC does not build affordable housing, but rather partners with other developers who do affordable housing. 3CDC manages multiple public properties, including Fountain Square and Washington Park.

Coded Language: A tactic of gentrification that includes words, phrases, or titles presented with the intention of persuading the viewer. Examples, such as, "Building Life in the City" by a developer, is an attempt to create positive feelings, regardless of the community impact.

Community Benefits Agreement (CBA): A mediation resulting in a legally binding document wherein multiple parties reach an agreement regarding expectations of roles, responsibilities, and financial support.

Community Development Corporations (CDC): Community organizations, often non-profit, who provide input and guide development in communities. Many CDC's land bank, and there are concerns that some may displace low-income residents. Additional community concerns includes making decisions without community input, pushing development without stopping displacement, and getting backroom deals at city hall, among others.

Corporate Welfare: Any public good (i.e. a financial investment, real estate, or tax incentive) that is awarded to a private entity, such as a corporation or developer. Corporate welfare can also concern the interwoven roles of business in politics.

Criminalization of Homelessness: People who are experiencing homelessness are often arrested or harassed by police for doing typical things that one might do at home. For instance, the lack of public restrooms may result in a person experiencing homelessness receiving a ticket or jailed for using the bathroom in an alley. This ticket or arrest can result in fines and more issues with the criminal legal system, furthering the cycle of poverty. Other types of criminalization include labeling everyone in the neighborhood or those who use a specific park as "the criminal element," accelerating evictions with nuisance property designations, double standards about who can consume alcohol, and hostile policing that results in harassment. Criminalization of homelessness can also include loitering or vagrancy laws.

Denial of Experience: Denial of experience can be seen when assertions are made about your neighborhood that contradict your own experience, often with intent to persuade. It is a tactic of gentrification.

Direct Gentrification: When residents, businesses, institutions, etc., are directly removed from their location. This could be done through eviction, raising rent, non-renewal of lease, remodeling, rising costs, other legal avenues, or by creating an otherwise unlivable circumstance.

Discomfort: A tactic of gentrification used to increase indirect gentrification by making a neighborhood unlivable for long-term and low-income residents. Examples include the removal of public park areas and privatizing parks because of safety concerns; telling people they aren't important, that the market is more important than the residents; creating businesses that are hostile to long-term residents; replacing sidewalks with seating for private business; increasingly loud events and features, such as a peddle wagon and bands/flea markets in public parks.

Disinvestment: Willful denial of public funding for streets, sidewalks, streetlights, schools, parks, pools, etc., while prioritizing funding for projects with the greatest return on the investment or are politically expeditious.

Displacement: Removing residents and/or small businesses from their place of origin. Displacement is seen in raising rents and in the increasing number evictions. The total number of residents can decrease even as an influx of new residents is experienced. Displacement can also occur from parks, schools, sidewalks, streets, etc., and it's often with the goal of a different class of people returning to that space.

Dog Parks and Breweries: A tactic of gentrification that privatizes or reduces public access to public areas. Examples include gating off public alleys for private events, or permanently; replacing park patrons with narrowly defined activities, such as dog parks, spray grounds, etc.; giving benefits to breweries, such as reduced water costs, that are not afforded to other businesses, like laundromats.

Double Standard: When rules or laws apply to certain groups of people but not to others.

Down Da Way: A nickname given to Over-the-Rhine and parts of the West End, Mt. Auburn, Downtown, and CUF by Black residents. Mainly describing the physical location of the urban basin, which is geographically lower than the rest of the city, and is connected to neighborhoods surrounding Over-the-Rhine.

False Narrative: Making a claim about an area, a group of people, or a building that is intended to reframe or redefine the historical record outside of a larger context. Claiming neighborhoods or amenities within the neighborhood are dangerous, undesirable, unsafe, to *depress then invest* in the area, is a false narrative. Saying certain people don't deserve to live in a specific area, such as low-income families don't deserve to live around an updated park, is a false narrative. Claims about the revitalization of the neighborhood often leave out the impact on long-term and low-income residents.

Favoring Businesses over Residents: Using metrics and data from developers and other businesses to validate decisions while minimizing the negative impact on residents.

Forced Programming: A tactic of gentrification, forced programming is the reclaiming public spaces with programming, such as concerts, workouts, flea markets, etc., to force the park's typical users out of the area, whether temporarily or permanently.

Gentrification: Removal of people, places, community culture, etc., aided by governmental subsidies and corporate welfare, largely benefiting the wealthy class at the expense of Black and long-term residents, ultimately restricting access for low-income and long-term residents while simultaneously increasing access and comfort for wealthy, connected, typically (but not limited to) beneficiaries of white generational wealth and capital.

Homeless: Not having a fixed, or regular, place to live or sleep. Some examples include living doubled up, couch surfing, living in a shelter, on the street, or with limited legal protection.

Housing First: A model that provides supportive services to people who move from homelessness to a home. The housing model provides services for people to address barriers often made worse by homelessness, like mental health barriers and addictions, by providing necessary support and community connections once a person has housing. Housing First is a low-barrier model, as sobriety is not required for housing, for instance.

Hostile Design: Things to prevent people from doing normal things, like walking, sitting, standing, congregating, or laying down in public places. Some auditory examples include mosquito boxes in alleys and classical music playing outside of a corner store. Some physical examples include benches with bars in the middle to prevent laying down, benches that are removed or too small to lay down, or even spikes, fences, sloped surfaces, and planter boxes, all to stop someone from standing, sitting, or laying down. Hostile design exists in public spaces such as parks, but it also includes areas easily accessible to the public, such as sidewalks and stoops.

Housing Protections: Legal and administrative protections that ensure individuals and families have the right to housing. Legal protections often lack executive enforcement, which leaves households without redress or relief. Organizations like Housing Opportunities Made Equal (HOME) and Legal Aid provide housing protection services, but more can be done legislatively. Cities can adopt pay-to-stay ordinances, create housing courts that are mediated between tenants and landlords that prevent eviction, enact just-cause eviction protections, and more.

Impaction Ordinance: 2001 Cincinnati legislation that restricted the building of new low-income housing in areas impacted by high rates of poverty. This vague policy created restrictions on the building of new housing and the inclusion of social services in neighborhoods with high poverty rates, such as Over-the-Rhine.

Indirect Gentrification: A cultural shift in the community results in a power change that creates an unwelcoming atmosphere for long-term residents. Examples include losing mom and pop housing, stores, laundromats, post office, hardware stores, public pools, barbershops, family/friends, schools, etc. Former business and housing is replaced by upscale boutiques, market rate housing and condos, and expensive restaurants that mark-up the cost of typical food once found in the neighborhood shops (such chicken and waffles, fried chicken, BBQ, hot dogs, trendy canned beer, etc.), making the neighborhood itself unlivable.

Lack of Historical Insight: Claiming the process of pushing people out of the neighborhood is "progress" and that it benefits "us all," when people can't benefit from goods and services outside of their budget, or that they can't benefit from the "rising" neighborhood once they have been pushed out. A lack of historical insight can also be seen in increased calls for police presence and zero-tolerance policing models that have harmed the Black community.

Land Banking: When developers or speculators acquire property with the intent of waiting until the property is economically profitable to renovate. Land banking can result in neglected properties and an increase in litter and unsafe building conditions.

Neoliberalism: A social, political, and economic theory that claims that an unregulated market is the best economic model, while at the same time relying on public support to ensure the model's success. Examples of neoliberalism can be seen in the duplication of existing public services, such as street cleaning, trash removal, park management, parking facilities, etc., in which private organizations receive public funding but keep the user-generated fees. Neoliberalism is often seen as a model where the public takes the risk (i.e. makes the investment, gives up control of the land, and/or allows a reduction in payments now, in hopes of increased payments in the future), and the private receives the gain (i.e. public funding, public property, property taxes, density variances, height variances, tax forgiveness, etc., on top of the user fees). Although neoliberalism is often thought to be solely about the free market, it relies heavily on corporate welfare.

Operation Vortex: An aggressive policing strategy employed by the City in 2006 with cooperation from other agencies, resulting in the criminalization of Black residents by enforcing zero-tolerance policies in select areas, such as Over-the-Rhine, but not in white areas. Data has demonstrated that such policies unfairly target Black residents, and the strategy has had questionable results.

Over-the-Rhine: A historic neighborhood immediately north of the central business district in Cincinnati known for its rich immigrant history, including German brewing. Mainly built between 1850-1900, it contains a mix of historic Italianate architecture and new infill. Factors, such as the great migration and urban renewal have led to Over-the-Rhine's heavy Black and Appalachian population. Since 2000, the population has continued to decline overall, with more than half of the Black residents pushed from the neighborhood.

Over-the-Rhine People's Movement: People, organizations, and actions in Over-the-Rhine and neighboring areas that work together to increase community cohesiveness, reduce isolation, ensure housing stability, and fight for community self-determination.

Paternalism: A tactic of gentrification that includes actions and intentions that assert power over individuals, groups of people, or communities, often presented as altruistic. Examples of paternalism include:

- **Blight Removal, Neighborhood Enhancement Projects, Housing Court:** Judgements used as an excuse to remove low-income homeowners, privatize public spaces, etc.; anonymous reporting of code violations and a housing court that results in criminal proceedings; coded language;

- **Entrepreneurship programs:** Creating capital out of low-income residents, having shareholders take and "invest" in the ideas and creativities of people of color and other minority groups;

- **Surveillance:** Increased use of security cameras, police foot patrols, block watch programs, etc.

Person-first Language: Using language that focuses on the individual instead of their circumstance. For example, rather than saying a "homeless person" or "houseless people," person-first language puts the person's humanity first, recognizing that homelessness is a condition that someone is experiencing, and not a fixed or rigid identity. Instead, using language like a "person experiencing homelessness" or a "family living outdoors" is using person-first language. Using person-first language is also a way to be an advocate.

Portland Loo: A self-contained bathroom, often with external water access, that is operable year-round. A Portland Loo can be found at Smale Riverfront Park, at the base of Elm Street, but could be utilized throughout the city.

Privatization: Using public funds, resources, or laws to give aid or subsidy for private gain and/or control. Privatization often results in the loss of public amenities and introduces barriers to public participation. When things are privatized, it can be difficult to return them to public control.

Public Goods: Includes publicly controlled assets, such as land and financing, and intangible things like abatements, variances, and other tax benefits.

Redlining: Redlining is named after the Home Ownership Loan Corporation's (HOLC) historical practice of placing red lines on maps around neighborhoods that were considered risky investments, simply because these neighborhoods contained any Black residents. Redlining is also used to refer to contemporary and current practices that regulate Black residents to second-class, or lowered citizenship, by severely limiting access to governmentally sponsored programs and private capital. Today, redlining can refer to any type of barrier, typically racism, that forces segregated facilities or denies access to housing, medical care, transportation, banking, employment, clean water, clean air, etc.

Renaming: Naming areas, such as alleyways, sections of neighborhoods, etc., to distinguish from other parts of the neighborhood.

Rental Assistance Demonstration Project (RAD): A tool for housing authorities to gain access to private investment for housing. RAD conversions allow for an acceptable loss of units, the loss of right to return through demolition, and loss of tenant power. RAD is built upon the neoliberal ideology that because the federal government has underfunded public housing for so long, that only private resources and lending will be able to provide needed housing improvements. CMHA has already started using RAD and plans to use it more in the future.

Restrictive Covenants: Also known as deed restrictions, restrictive covenants can stipulate specific conditions for the property inside of the deed. They were used by the HOLC to restrict future sales to non-white residents. Restrictive covenants were often used to restrict the race of residents before the Fair Housing Act of 1968, but they can also be used to ensure future use of properties, such as restricting it to affordable housing.

Tax Benefits: Programs such as the Low-Income Housing Tax Credit (LIHTC), New Market Tax Credits, Historic Tax Credits, Tax-Increment Financing (TIF), and the city's Notice of Funding Availability (NOFA) program provide up-front construction financing for developers. Tax abatements are long-term property tax reductions that are awarded to developers when properties are renovated. A Special Improvement District (SID) is a state designation that allows additional property taxes from an area to be collected and distributed to a service organization to provide public services. Tax benefits are often both an example of corporate welfare and neoliberalism.

Urban Renewal: Federal and local policies that resulted in the mass displacement of residents, generally beginning in the 1950's with the interstate system.

STUDY QUESTIONS

Chapter 1: Background on Cincinnati History

1. What parallels can be made between the Native American experience and the early colonists, with Black residents of Kenyon Barr and urban renewal? What parallels can also be seen with the long-term residents of Over-the-Rhine and the current wave of gentrification?

2. How has the history of Cincinnati failed to honor the legacy of the laborers and trades people who created so much wealth in the region? Why does Cincinnati fall behind its peer cities on measures of equity? What can the city do to address these issues?

3. How does concentrated suburban white wealth pose a threat to the livelihoods of long-term Black residents in the city?

4. How has the Great Depression impacted housing today? How did the Great Depression impact where you grew up and where you plan to live in the future?

5. What did you find surprising about the history of Cincinnati? What do you think should be included in a traditional history class? What do you think was omitted from your own history classes? Why?

Chapter 2: Displacement in a Changing Neighborhood

1. How does displacement affect a community? What issues might displacement cause for a family who has been forced out?

2. What impact does hostile design have on access to public spaces? In what ways does hostile design contradict our commonly held notion of freedom in America?

3. What does the language of gentrification look like? Sound like? Who is often omitted from the conversation about gentrification? How is the language of gentrification different from person-first language?

4. What is a double standard? How are double standards placed on people experiencing homelessness? In what ways do double standards result in the criminalization of homelessness?

5. How does privatization impact access to neighborhood amenities? In what ways could the city require public access to privatized properties, such as parks?

Chapter 3. Power Factors in the Community

1. In what ways do systems, political, social, environmental, etc., perpetuate homelessness and poverty? What are some specific examples? In what ways could these systems be challenged?

2. Many low-income long-term residents are facing increased pressure that is forcing them from their homes. In what ways can tenants work together to fight back against gentrification? Can you name a specific time this was successful?

3. Although gentrification often leads to subjectively better-looking areas, mainly due to investment, what are some issues that gentrification creates in a neighborhood? What specific power imbalances are created when governmental bodies provide financing to private developers?

4. How have large corporations, such as sports teams, displaced residents in Cincinnati? Who was displaced, and who is at risk? Why do you think the story of displacement is often buried in the news, rather than shown in the light?

5. What is the result of displacement from public spaces? How have Findlay Playground and Imagination Alley shown us the result of privatization and displacement? How might displacement increase isolation, loneliness, and depression?

Chapter 4: System Loss of Community Cohesion

1. What are social ties? Why are social ties important to people in your community? How are social ties lost through gentrification? What is the result?

2. Name a singularity. Explain how things changed due to this singularity and how it would be impossible to return to the way things were before. How has this singularity impacted poverty or homelessness?

3. How do social movements intersect? Specifically, discuss how the movement to eradicate homelessness relates to the anti-poverty movement. Are there other ways that the movement to eradicate homelessness intersects with other social movements? If so, which ones? Explain how they intersect.

4. How are police used to further the goal of gentrification? How does policing increase the criminalization of homelessness? Describe an alternative to policing, specific to homelessness.

5. What are some of the authors political stances? How are they similar or different from your own?

Chapter 5: Homelessness and Gentrification

1. What are the main causes of homelessness? How do stereotypes impact the ways in which people both understand the causes of homelessness and the solutions to ending homelessness? How do factors such as age, race, gender, and sexual orientation interact with wealth and income inequality? How do these factors impact an individual's or family's likelihood of homelessness?

2. What is the appropriate way to interact with someone who is panhandling? Why does human connection matter to you?

3. What are some specific struggles that people who are experiencing homelessness deal with daily that people who have housing take for granted? How would limitations on you impact your abilities?

4. Why are Black residents of Cincinnati more likely to experience homelessness as compared to their white peers? How do you think the constant threat

of homelessness impacts all aspects of their lives, including education, health, transportation, recreation, and family cohesion?

5. Why is the criminalization of homelessness ineffective at addressing the root causes of homelessness? What are the root causes of homelessness? Name specific ways in which gentrification fails to address these causes.

Activity: Tactics of Gentrification: Photographic Neighborhood Assessment

1. What did you find difficult about this exercise? What did you find surprising?

2. Which items from your list were you able to find? Why do you think these items represented the topics on your list?

3. How do you think these items might impact the lived experience of long-term residents in the neighborhood?

4. Which items were you unable to find on your list? Do you think items like that exist in the neighborhood? What might a plan to find these items look like? If you found all your items, name something else that you found that you might add to your list.

5. Considering that each item makes up a larger whole, what items on your list do you feel are for tourists in the neighborhood, rather than long-term residents? Do you think this is fair? Why or why not? Please consider access issues, like cost and comfort, in your answer.

ACKNOWLEDGMENTS

I would like to express my deepest gratitude to the Greater Cincinnati Homeless Coalition staff, speakers, volunteers, board, and supporters who have helped me with both my work and my reflective writing. They each have given support, feedback, inspiration, information, perspective, and inspiration to complete this work. I am honored to help share in the work of the Over-the-Rhine People's Movement, which inspires me to remain engaged in this work.

Thanks should also go to the founders of the Over-the-Rhine People's Movement and the Greater Cincinnati Homeless Coalition, including buddy gray.

I could not have completed this work without the contribution of the Forward by Alice Skirtz, and without the Editors of *Streetvibes*, who have encouraged me and helped me to determine article content.

I am also grateful to all the students, teachers, professors, schools, universities, church groups, social service organizations, and individuals, who have participated in our education program who enliven my spirit and continue the work of creating a more empathetic community. I cannot begin to express my thanks to Chris Wilkey and Brian Bailie for their enthusiastic support of this work.

I gratefully acknowledge the assistance of Nick Raymond, Shirley Phillips, and phrie for their help structuring and providing feedback on this work.

Finally, I would like to thank my community, my neighbors, families, and my partner, Key Beck, for their profound contributions and their belief in the importance of the work that I do.

Thank you!

ABOUT THE AUTHOR

Dr. Mark, a Cincinnati native, earned his PhD in Educational Studies from the University of Cincinnati. At the University of Cincinnati, he is also received a Master of Education in Educational Foundations with certificates in Peace Studies and Urban Educational Leadership. His undergrad focused on information design, production, and education, as he earned a Bachelor of Philosophy in Interdisciplinary Studies from the Western College Program at Miami University, Oxford, Ohio. Dr. Mark is a graduate of Walnut Hills High School.

Advised and aided by Drs. Marvin Berlowitz, Vanessa Allen-Brown, Roger Collins, Steve Carlton-Ford, Wei Pan, and Rodney Coates, Dr. Mark's dissertation focused on measuring and evaluating trust in the classroom, specifically in relation to advertising and commercialism in schools. During graduate school, Dr. Mark held many leadership positions and continued to volunteer in the community, including at the Peaslee Neighborhood Center and the Drop Inn Center. After receiving his PhD, Dr. Mark worked for several years as a GED instructor before working with the Greater Cincinnati Homeless Coalition as the Director of Education.

At the Homeless Coalition, Dr. Mark has produced educational materials and expanded the program to include trainings and tours about gentrification, homelessness, and privatization. Dr. Mark also runs the Speaker's Bureau, which provides opportunities for people who have experienced homelessness to earn money while increasing the empathy of the audience. The Greater Cincinnati Homeless Coalition's education program reaches thousands of people each year and is an essential way for people to learn more about their own role in homelessness and how they can work to eradicate homelessness.

Each of the included essays has been printed in *Streetvibes* newspaper. Dr. Mark selected each of these articles out of more than 125 articles that he has written for *Streetvibes* because they directly relate to gentrification, displacement, privatization, poverty, homelessness, and Over-the-Rhine. These articles are intended to present a street level view of these issues as they presented themselves over a period of four years from the autumn of 2015 through 2019.

www.ingramcontent.com/pod-product-compliance
Lightning Source LLC
Chambersburg PA
CBHW021856230426
43671CB00006B/417